THE
BOXER'S STORY

THE BOXER'S STORY

FIGHTING FOR MY LIFE IN THE NAZI CAMPS

NATHAN SHAPOW

WITH BOB HARRIS

The Robson Press

First published in Great Britain in 2012 by
The Robson Press (an imprint of Biteback Publishing Ltd)
Westminster Tower
3 Albert Embankment
London SE1 7SP

Copyright © Nathan Shapow and Bob Harris 2012

Nathan Shapow and Bob Harris have asserted their rights under the Copyright,
Designs and Patents Act 1988 to be identified as the authors of this work.

Plate section: images on pages 1, 4, 5 and 8 author's own;
images on page 2 © Bundesarchiv

Every reasonable effort has been made to trace copyright holders of material
reproduced in this book, but if any have been inadvertently overlooked the publishers
would be glad to hear from them.

ISBN 978-1-84954-190-9

10 9 8 7 6 5 4 3 2 1

A CIP catalogue record for this book is available from the British Library.

Set in Grotesque and Adobe Caslon Pro by Namkwan Cho
Cover design by Namkwan Cho

Printed and bound in Great Britain by
CPI Group (UK) Ltd, Croydon CR0 4YY

CONTENTS

ACKNOWLEDGEMENTS

Nathan Shapow and Bob Harris would like to acknowledge the unstinting help of Nathan's wife Hela Shapow, his daughter Adina and especially his son Mike, whose enthusiasm got the show on the road, as well as the late Isidor Nussenbaum, Shulam Sorkin, Annette Segal and Bob's sounding boards, David Pleat and Jonny Dexter. Special thanks also go to Bob's literary agent, Robert Smith, and last, but by no means least, a massive hand to Jeremy Robson and his excellent staff at the Robson Press, including designer Namkwan Cho for his brilliant cover and painstaking editor Reuben Cohen.

FOREWORD

From time to time, even in the life of a professional writer accustomed to tales of heroism and
extraordinary stamina, one comes across a story so
powerful and emotive that it forces you to question
your own values, makes the world seem a very different place. It has been my great fortune, as a veteran
sportswriter, to meet many of the world's outstand-
ing athletes, to recount the tales of lives devoted to
competition, struggle and victory – often heroic in
their own ways. But Nathan Shapow's heroism, for all
that it stemmed in some part from athletic prowess
and great talent as a boxer, was of a different order.

We hear so often of the Holocaust, and the approx-
imately six million Jews slaughtered by the Nazis, that
it is easy to forget they were not some homogene-
ous mass of victims without names, but individuals.

Rabbis, lawyers, writers, artists, scientists, children, atheists and the deeply religious: the Jewish victims of the Holocaust were human beings, as were those who survived. The stories of survivors are always moving, inspirational stories of evading the brutal Nazi genocide that the late Pope John Paul II argued proved the existence of Satan. Amongst them is the story of Nathan Shapow – or 'Nachke' to his comrades – a Riga-born Jew who fought for his life in the Latvian Ghetto, a series of concentration camps, and went on to fight for the creation of the State of Israel.

It was through my friendship with his son Mike that I was introduced to Nathan, and to the idea of writing his book. I travelled to Los Angeles for an initial discussion and, as politely and discreetly as I could, asked about his experiences in the war. 'You don't want to know,' he would answer. I learned that this had often been his answer, too, to Mike and Adina, his daughter. But slowly, over time, he began to speak of what he'd been through, in Latvia, Germany, France and the battle for Israel's independence. It is a story of such strength and defiance in the face of overwhelming force and evil that at times, I found it difficult to believe. Nathan faced death time and time again – as a prisoner, a warrior, and for the simple reason of his being Jewish – and his story was, as the reader will see, one of such fortitude and a stubborn will to live that my journalistic instincts led me to check some of his claims. To my amazement, it transpired that if anything, he had understated the extent of what he'd been through and the bravery with which he fought, not just for his own survival, but to protect and save as many of his fellow Jews as he could. No wonder he was known as 'The Strong One' – or, in Yiddish, *Shtarker*. The latter strikes me as by far the better word, as it echoes the English word 'stark': and Nathan's strength, deployed in battle amidst the starkest times of modern history, manifested in stark, dark terms indeed.

I am a sportswriter, not a historian – and this is not a work of academic history. It is one man's story, which touched on many other lives, and a story that has yet to end, for Nathan, now in his nineties, still lives in California, in proximity to the Hollywood producers and directors who would surely jump at such a story if it were presented to them as a novel.

However, this is not fiction, but one man's extraordinary story, told from memory, not an attempt to record the whole history of the Holocaust in Latvia and beyond, nor the creation of the State of Israel. It is the story of a family man who lost his mother and two brothers to the cruelties of Nazism and communism, a man who fought back, embodying the famous words of Winston Churchill: 'Never give up. Never give up. Never, never, never give up.' His persistence and courage were the traits of a true hero, but, for all the tragedy he lived through, not a tragic one: his marriage, children, grandchildren and great-grandchildren attest to his triumph, and it is my great privilege to have been granted access to his life story, with all its twists and turns.

Nathan Shapow said nothing of the story in these pages till late in a long, ongoing life: although I did not, for a long time, think myself to be the appropriate author of such a work, it has been an honour and a life-changing experience to hear and help him tell his story. It is an epic of survival, and gentile that I am, an epic that has helped me understand why Israel fights, continually, to preserve the achievements of Nathan and his comrades, the men and women who walked from the gates of Bergen-Belsen and Auschwitz, traumatised and wounded, and went on to fight, securing their own nation-state.

There will, no doubt, be errors and mistakes, most of them mine, within this book, but I have no doubt that the story of Nathan Shapow, The Strong One, is a true – and truly remarkable – odyssey.

Bob Harris, 2012

CHAPTER ONE

MURDER IN THE GHETTO

For more than sixty years I kept the secret, telling no one. Not Hela, my beloved wife, a survivor of Auschwitz and Belsen, nor our children Mike and Adina. I never breathed a word of it, not to those I loved most, or those who would have surely understood, my fellow concentration camp survivors, amongst them many of my closest friends in our adopted country, the United States.

I have always been open about the fact I killed as a soldier in Israel's War of Independence and the young state's battles with her neighbours, fighting the British, the Arabs of Palestine and their allies. Such is the collateral damage of any war. What I kept to myself until now was the day, long before I had seen Israel or America, when I committed murder; cold-blooded and premeditated murder.

Obersturmführer Hoffman was a self-important SS officer who took great delight in beating defenceless Jews in the Riga Ghetto. For some reason, I was amongst his favourite targets. Perhaps he could not stand to see my attitude, for I neither looked nor felt like the Nazi's stereotype of the 'racially inferior, degenerate Jew'. I was young, strong as an ox from years of football, swimming and boxing, and carried myself like an athlete. Though imprisoned in the Ghetto, a slave labourer, I was not cowed, despite being incarcerated in my home city by a foreign army which wanted nothing less than world domination and the 'liquidation' of the Jews. By October of 1941, just months after the Nazis came to Latvia, over 30,000 Jews had already been murdered. Those of us still alive had been selected to first serve the Nazis as slave labourers, before we joined the dead.

I had survived so far for the very same reason that Obersturmführer Hoffman loathed me with such passion. I was known as 'Nachke', a *Shtarker*, one of the so-called 'strong ones' in the Latvian Jewish Ghetto, strong from years of training as a boxer in the Jewish sporting organisation Maccabi and the Zionist Youth Movement Beitar. Before they could 'eliminate' all Baltic Jews, the Nazis used those of us they could as disposable slave labour, and my years of sport made me useful when it came to shifting lumber, breaking rubble, loading and unloading supply trains. But staying strong meant staying healthy –

which, in the Ghetto, was possible only by way of stealing food.

The camp authorities provided us with bare subsistence rations, a daily quarter slice of bread and a 'soup' of lukewarm water flavoured with potatoes. It was hardly enough to live on, let alone to keep the strength required to work twelve-hour shifts of back-breaking physical labour, under the watchful eyes of German guards and Kapos – the lowest of the low, treacherous Jews and Latvians who policed the camps. They were prisoners themselves but, in return for informing on and beating inmates, received better rations than the rest of us, and gifts of alcohol and cigarettes. The Kapos were encouraged to be brutal in administering 'discipline' in the camps: many were criminals, rapists, murderers and sadists, released from Riga's jails by the Gestapo and selected for their violent natures. They often seemed determined to prove themselves more brutal than their SS overseers.

Inmates who grew too weak to work at the speed demanded by our German masters would be shot on the spot: but to steal food could bring punishments ranging from a beating by the guards or Kapos to summary execution. When the Kapos reported me for stealing crusts of bread, it was Hoffman who ordered my punishment, often beating me himself. His weapon of choice was an SS favourite, a rod of iron encased in rubber, but I knew it was only a matter of time before he tired of me and put a gun to my head.

In that environment, with death an ever-present threat, my senses were heightened by my will to survive, sharpened as I watched and listened to the guards and Kapos, a watchfulness that gave me an advantage, as did my natural ear for languages. I spoke not only the native Latvian tongue sometimes known as Lettish, but also Russian, Hebrew, Yiddish, a little English, and, like most Latvian Jews, good German. This was my secret weapon and I did not let my oppressors realise that I understood every word they said. Indeed, they thought their language was a mystery to Ghetto inmates, and freely discussed their plans in front of us.

On that fateful day, I knew Hoffman had decided to have done with me when I overheard him tell a fellow guard that I was stealing food from the mouths of German soldiers. That choice of words was telling, especially when he said that he intended to personally search my room in the Ghetto for contraband. I knew he meant to kill me. If he really wanted to have my room searched, he would have sent a guard or Kapo. No self-respecting Obersturmführer, an SS rank equivalent to that of Oberleutnant ('senior Lieutenant'), would soil his well-manicured hands with such a lowly task, and Hoffman did not lack for self-respect. He was a preening, arrogant man, even for an SS officer, and would have thought it quite below his dignity to search an inmate's room for food. I knew with perfect clarity that he was going to kill me ... or so he thought. But I was not about to die

4

without a fight, even though the odds were stacked heavily against me.

I comforted myself with the thought that Hoffman's belief that Jews were spineless vermin, unable to resist the 'Master Race', prevented him from bringing guards or Kapos with him for security. It was to be one on one, though not exactly a fair fight. Only one of us, after all, was armed: my empty, Jewish hands against an SS Luger.

'Raus,' he snapped, 'Du Juden Schwein.' ('Hurry, you Jewish pig.')

Hoffman was dressed immaculately in his officer's uniform, the SS insignia affixed to his shoulder, while I wore the paper-thin striped clothes of a prisoner, my light jacket emblazoned with the Star of David on the left breast, and on my back the word 'Jude' (Jew), prominently stretched across my shoulders, as was required of all Jews in the Ghetto. The Star of David, universal symbol of the Jews, marked us out as *untermenschen*, in fact, the very lowest of the 'races' in Nazi thought: an irony, as the Hebrew term for the Star, *Magen David* – The Shield of David – reflects the legend that King David bore the symbol into battle on his Shield. It was a proud emblem, and now adorns Israel's flag, but the Nazis had perverted its meaning, and the yellow stars of the Ghetto uniform would not shield me from Hoffman's gun.

'Schneller, Schneller ihr dreck Juden!' ('Faster, faster, you Jewish scum!')

The miserable weather, overcast and cold as rain fell from a sky the colour of ice, suddenly became a spectacle of beauty. The Rabbis say that those killed in the Holocaust died *al kiddush Hashem* – 'for the sanctification of the divine name' – but I was a fighter and, to me, to die at Hoffman's hands would have been a terrible dishonour. I wanted more, more sky, more rain, more sun, more life: a life beyond the Ghetto, freedom and a family of my own in the Promised Land.

As Hoffman marched me down the narrow streets at double-time, towards the tiny cell that had become my home, pushing me with his gloved hand whenever my pace slowed, I mentally prepared myself to throw what would be the most important punch of my life. There would be no second in my corner, no referee or bell, no victory on points or by a technical knockout. I had to put him down fast and quietly or it was over.

We arrived at the house and he hustled me to my door, closing it behind him and sliding the bolt shut. I could smell his strong cologne in the tight, enclosed space as his lips curled back in a feral snarl and he began to unbutton his holster. This was the moment. Die like a coward or die as a warrior. I took a step towards him, moving slowly, almost imperceptibly, and as his hand closed round the handle of his pistol, I let my training take hold. With all my strength and skill, I threw a fast, round-arm left hook, the punch that made a legend of Joe Frazier.

Boxers learn early on that the round-arm left hook can be both a devastating blow when used correctly and an excellent 'softener', setting up a knockout punch. Thrown at close range, it comes outside the opponent's field of vision and is difficult to defend against, even from a practised fighting stance. Reaching for his gun, Hoffman's guard was down, both literally and figuratively. The SS were accustomed to us Jews being subservient and fearful, obeying their orders and never fighting back. He was not prepared for my assault. Though a strong man and trained soldier, Hoffman was softened by rich meals the likes of which I could only dream of, not to mention the officer's reserve supply of vodka, schnapps and brandy. He was certainly no boxer, and my left hook was enough to stun him. I followed with a classic straight right, connecting with his chin, which had veered to the side from the force of my first punch, his mouth hanging open in shock and pain. I heard the crack of bone as Hoffman's Aryan jaw broke.

Down he went, his gun sliding from his holster as he slumped to the stone floor. Where was the arrogant SS officer now? His 'racial superiority' must have deserted him, as he lay helpless, struck down by a Jew. This time he was the one to take a beating.

In another world, another time, I would have stepped back to my own corner, confident the referee would count him out. But this was no tournament, and the Marquis of Queensbury rules did not apply.

There was no turning back. Had a Kapo or a German soldier passed by and stopped to investigate the noise, I would have been a dead man. If he recovered from my knockout blow I would not even live long enough to walk to the gallows in the infamous Blechplatz – 'Tin Square' – where many Jews had perished at the end of a hangman's rope. Indeed, had he been able to fight me off long enough to reach his weapon or call for help, Hoffman might well have ordered not just my execution, but the death of all my friends. That was the usual Nazi response to resistance.

I could not use his weapon to finish him off, as the pistol's report would have been loud enough to bring guards and Kapos running. In a frenzy, I looked around and grabbed a heavy wooden stool, hoisted it above my shoulders and steadied myself. I brought it down on his skull with all the power I could muster and heard, again, the cracking of bone. He died in an instant, his skull crushing inwards. It was a quicker death than he deserved, but a lucky one from my perspective, as very little blood was spilled.

I stood there for a second, regaining my breath and trying to accept what had just happened. I had killed my nemesis. He had come to murder me and I had turned the tables on him. But there was no time to take satisfaction in this victory; with every passing second the threat to my life grew. I forced myself to stay calm and think the situation through. It was early evening and everyone, Latvians, Germans, Jews alike, was out of the Ghetto on work detail. But they would soon be back. I had to dispose of the evidence.

I slipped quietly out through the door and looked up and down the damp cobbled streets: there was no one in sight. Short, stocky and strong as I was, I had no trouble lifting his inert body, hooking my arms under his shoulders and dragging him out of the house. Hoffman left a fitting monument to himself: a wet stain where he had voided his bowels as his brain caved in. I hauled him deep into the darkening streets, my ears alert for the slightest sound. I knew if I heard anyone approaching there would be no time to see if it was friend or foe. I would have to just drop the corpse where it was and disappear.

The further I took him away from my room the calmer I felt. At last, without ceremony or sympathy, I dumped him in a doorway several streets away.

Except for the distant rumble of an old tram car, it was silent as twilight spread through the Ghetto streets. The beating of my heart gradually returned to normal as a cooling rain washed sweat from my brow. Then I froze. His cap. His bloody cap. What had happened to his bloody peaked cap?

Forcing myself to keep a normal, walking pace – prisoners did not run in the Ghetto – I turned back towards the house. I was almost shaking when I burst into my room and began a frantic search for the grey cap with its death's head insignia. At that moment, it was every bit as much a lethal threat to me as

Hoffman's gun had been when he reached for it. And I could not see the wretched thing at first.

There. When he crashed to the ground, the hat had, naturally, fallen and rolled, coming to rest behind the cupboard. I grabbed it, stuffed it inside my shirt, and hastily checked that the coast was still clear. Off I went, and as soon as I reached a deserted corner I tossed it out into the night, like a kid skimming stones on the surface of the Baltic.

Once again, I drew a deep breath and set off for home, my mind racing at the enormity of what I'd done. But there were no regrets. It had been the starkest and most straightforward of choices: his life or mine. I had killed for the first time.

It would not be the last.

Back in my room, I cleaned away all remnants of the Obersturmführer. The little blood he'd lost was quickly wiped away with an old rag, which I then stuffed onto the smouldering fire in the grate, watching it flame and vanish. I hadn't realised just how much we'd bounced around in that small room. The few sticks of furniture were scattered across the floor and, on close examination, my three-legged stool, which had served so ably as a bludgeon, bore blood, skin and even hair on the edge that had struck Hoffman. I wiped the stool and rubbed it in the dirt to cover the traces of Hoffman's remains. I straightened everything else up as best I could, but a small bloodstain remained on the floor. It was noticeable to me, but the floor was old, filthy and covered in stains. I hoped and prayed that no one else would recognise it.

I kept the gun that he had planned to kill me with, and hid it, along with the ammunition, in our secret cellar. The door was concealed beneath a heavy cupboard, which normally required two pairs of hands to shift. In the past, I had been able to move it by myself, with effort. That day, it was easier than usual. The adrenalin was still flowing.

The gun joined our secret cache of contraband – stolen food, vodka, and other luxury items that we 'strong ones' had stolen, scavenged or bartered for in the Ghetto's black market. With our puny official rations, everything had its value, and the gun could be useful in our ongoing struggle. At first I thought that hiding it alongside the bottles and cans presented no extra risk – if the Germans came this close to discovering who had murdered Hoffman, they would have killed me in an instant. There would be no trial. The Ghetto did not enjoy the rule of law.

I was about to leave the dark, damp cellar when I realised that the gun would stick out like a sore thumb amongst our other treasures, prompting questions from the handful of people in my group who knew of our store. As much as I trusted them, who could tell what they might reveal under interrogation, or even torture? Why take the chance? The fewer people who knew, the less danger I faced, and if I kept both the gun and Hoffman's death to myself, then, I thought, there would be no risk at all. Time would show how wrong I was in this respect.

At that moment, all I could do was to hide the gun inside my private 'safe' – no bank vault, but a narrow space in the floor, beneath a couple of loose bricks. I lifted them out and, after studying the weapon closely, stroking and caressing it like a pet dog, I slid it into the hole, replaced the bricks and scattered dirt around their edges.

I had made two serious mistakes, and realised them just in time. A third could kill me. With Hoffman's body and hat disposed of and his gun hidden from Jews and guards alike, I made my way out into the night. It was fully dark now, and freezing. I shivered from both the cold and the terrifying thoughts of what might easily have happened if my first punch had not caught Hoffman cold, had a Kapo happened by and heard the struggle, had my luck not held as I got rid of the body.

It could – and by all laws of probability, it should – have been me lying dead with a bullet in my brain. Instead, it was that Nazi bastard. He would kill no more Jews. I began to relax a little as I joined up with a group of my fellow Jewish workers heading home, my head down, my collar high around my neck. If anyone noticed my sudden, strange appearance from the shadows, they gave no sign. This was a group from another block, but we were all fighting the same war.

☞

Early the next morning, Hoffman's body was found and the Ghetto was thrown into chaos. The SS could not believe that someone had dared to kill one of their officers. After all, they were the Master Race, and we were under their jackboots, living in fear. They never thought that we would even contemplate fighting back.

We were rounded up before dawn and lined up in rows of four in Blechplatz, in sight of the gallows. Hoffman's superior officer, SS-Sturmbannführer (a rank equivalent to that of Major) Kurt Krause, came out to question us. Had Krause himself been murdered, we were told in no uncertain terms, all the Jews in the Ghetto would have died that morning. I believed them.

Krause commanded the guards to find the guilty party. They pushed us, kicked us and screamed in our faces, demanding to know who had done this terrible deed. Their violent interrogation brought them nothing, simply because no one but me knew who had put an end to the life of that despicable man. The guards grew more and more irate as the prisoners' silence became sullen, with even the usually reliable informants having nothing to contribute. Eventually, Krause snapped. He bellowed out orders, turned on his heel and left with a flamboyant 'Heil Hitler' salute.

His response to our silence was to have two of my fellow Jews pulled from the line and marched over to the gallows. Their hands were tied behind their backs and both were promptly hanged in front of us. I thought that I had long since forgotten how to cry, but tears ran down my cheeks as I watched these innocent men scream and struggle while the guards wrestled them up onto the gallows, tied nooses round their necks and released the trapdoors.

The screams died in their throats as they jerked and flapped about, their hands clutching and clawing at the air behind their backs in spasms, their blackening tongues lolling out obscenely. Gradually, their movements ceased. The guards, flustered and furious at the loss of their officer, herded us off to our days' duties as dawn broke overhead.

The two hanged men were left dangling for the next three days as a warning of the consequences of resistance. To me, they were a constant reminder that I had caused their deaths. I was devastated by the murder of my comrades, and had to fight my conscience to stop myself from running and confessing everything to the Sturmbannführer. I would have done so when they questioned us, had I thought it would save lives, but there was little or no chance of that amidst the fury of the SS at the murder of their Lieutenant. Proportionate responses were not the SS way and others would have died, even had I offered myself up to the gallows.

I felt nothing for Hoffman, my torturer and would-be killer, but the guilt over the two men who died owing to my actions has tormented me ever since. I still see their lifeless bodies swinging in the wind as I walked past Tin Square on my way to work, my guilty secret bottled up inside me. I knew I was right to have killed Hoffman ... but at such a cost? The first time I passed those dangling bodies I gave them the briefest of glances and came close to vomiting, the bile rising in my throat. They were dead because of me.

I wasn't brave enough to look at them again, and kept my head down and my eyes averted every time I walked through Blechplatz until they were cut down, making way for other victims. Their images were imprinted on my mind in terrible and vivid detail, and have remained with me for more than half a century.

This is the first time I have ever told this story, and although the memory brings fresh tears to my eyes, I feel great relief at having spat it out, like the poison it is. Maybe the nightmare of seeing my innocent comrades executed will fade a little now ... or is that hoping for too much? I feel better for having at last got this off my chest, but still, I lack the courage to name the men who died in my place because their families, if any relatives of either man survive, would never forgive me. How could they?

It is easy, in retrospect, to condemn me, to brand me a coward, but before you judge me too harshly, let me remind you of the circumstances, not as an excuse, but an explanation. Tens of thousands of Latvian Jews had been murdered by the SS and their Latvian allies by the time I was moved into the Kleine, or small, Riga Ghetto, which held a few thousand Latvian Jews: while the houses of the Grosse (large) Ghetto were filled with German Jews, after their original inhabitants were gunned down in the forests. Imagine a dozen streets in your home town being suddenly cordoned off, people driven out and others moved in. No families, no husbands and wives living with their children as we take for granted now, just men and women herded together and left to wonder what had happened to their relatives, their homes and possessions.

When the German Jews were shipped in, they were given preferential treatment and allowed to remain together as families, moving into houses in the Big Ghetto, finding half-eaten meals on kitchen tables abandoned by the Latvian Jews as they were marched out to the woods of Bikernieki or Rumbula to die terrible deaths.

A few survived the initial slaughter, hiding when the Germans and Kapos swept through the streets, clearing them before raising the barbed wire fences, but the incoming German Jews quickly discovered them. Most were turned over, but a few were secreted away, looked after by their fellow Jews and smuggled back into our Ghetto. Prisoners were shot and hanged each day. I was still a young man, with so much to do, and when it came to the question of kill or be killed, I acted from instinct.

It was him or me, and I have lived with the consequences, the guilt, the nightmares, ever since. I was not born into the Ghetto, and my refusal to die there allowed me, in time, to bring children into the world, to fight for Israel, to live a full and varied life, a life denied to most Jews in the Baltics. But there had been life, too, before the Nazis came, life with a family – my family – that had been happy, once, in Latvia, until the war tore us apart.

CHAPTER TWO

A BRIEF CHILDHOOD

I was born on 6 November 1921, to my father Mordechai and my mother Chaye, the first of their three sons. My brother Boris was a year younger than me and I was a full thirteen years older than the baby of the family, Ephraim, or 'Fima', as we called him. We lived in a simple house on two floors, with a kitchen and two bedrooms. We boys slept in one and my parents took the other. It was all we knew and more than enough for us; more by far than Jews in Latvia had traditionally known.

Modern Latvia was created after the First World War, following centuries of foreign rule and a long battle for independence. First, the region was occupied by the German Knightly Orders, who founded Riga in 1201 and forcibly converted the native Pagan population to Christianity, with the support of both the German King and Vatican. The German Knights prohibited all Jewish settlement in the area in 1306, a ban that lasted until 1561, when the country was divided into Lithuanian, German and Russian-dominated regions. A Jewish colony was founded in Piltene in the sixteenth century, and Jews played an important part in Latvia's development. But only prominent and wealthy Jews were allowed to live in Riga, and they could not be buried in the Riga City Limits until 1725, with bodies sent to Polish territory.

Thousands of Jews died in the terrible Great Northern War of 1700-1721, which ended with all of Latvia under Tsarist control. Those Jews outside the Russian Pale of settlement could only live in certain areas, and were forced to pay higher tax rates than the gentiles. In 1724, Jews were expelled from the Russian Empire by Empress Katherine. Only in 1785 did Catherine the Great lift the ban on Jewish settlement along the Baltic Coast, and it was not until 1841 that the Russian Senate granted Jews living in Riga an official right of residence. The Russian Empire was a century behind the rest of Europe, when it came to the emancipation of the Jews, and even the foundation of a free Latvian Republic did not bring true equality. Latvia's nationalist government kept a firm hand on the economy through a Tsarist-style civil service, and Jews were not permitted to attain high office or professional status.

Still, the inter-war years were a time of freedom and excitement, compared to what had gone before and Jewish life in Riga thrived. A once 'backwards' Jewish community, as in Russia, became cosmopolitan, internationalist and freed from religious orthodoxy. Latvian Jews made an important contribution to the growing Zionist movement, which sought to establish a Jewish State in Biblical Palestine. At that time, the British were still in control of Palestine, with some 100,000 troops stationed there. The British Mandate had been created by the League of Nations in 1920, following the collapse of the Ottoman Empire. Under the Mandate, Jewish habitation was restricted to a relatively small area, the lion's share (more than double) being used by the British to create a new Arab Protectorate which they called Transjordan (later the Arab Kingdom of Jordan). The Golan Heights, in the North, were ceded to the French Mandate of Syria, and the Southern part of the Mandate – the Negev desert – was also closed to Jewish settlement

Riga was the birthplace of Beitar, the right-wing youth movement devoted to the militant Zionist ideals of Vladimir Ze'ev Jabotinsky. His school of revisionist Zionism, hated by the socialist-Zionist majority, maintained that a Jewish State could only be won and kept by force. Beitar, founded in 1923 in Riga, promoted boxing, the study of Hebrew, urging its members to move to then-British mandate Palestine and join the fight for independence, teaching the use of small arms and techniques of guerrilla warfare. The Likud Party and the militias many of its members fought in – the Irgun and Stern Gang – were all born of Jabotinsky and Beitar.

My father was an early admirer of Jabotinsky and the Revisionist party, encouraging me to join Beitar as a young boy. They would prove crucial influences throughout my life in Latvia and later Israel. My father was originally a hat-maker, hence the name 'Shapov', Russian for 'hat', pronounced like the French *chapeau*. But he was also something of an entrepreneur, and turned his hand to money-changing, a decent trade in what remained a popular vacation spot with tourists from across Russia and Europe. He offered good rates of exchange, and became quite successful. We weren't rich but we were comfortable. Poppa earned enough for my mother to stay at home, dress fashionably and look after us children. An attractive brunette with beautiful hair, momma thoroughly enjoyed an active social life, and poppa joined her when he could. She even had her jewels, while we boys wanted for very little.

Like most children around the world in the days before television and video games, my chief interest was sport. Football was popular with all the lads of Riga, and I was no exception. I would have liked to play in goal, but had inherited my father's solid build, and was thought too heavy to be a goalkeeper. I played centre forward, in matches with many friends, both Jewish and Gentile, like Danny, a tall and powerful Slav, who had a Czechoslovakian father and a German mother. Along with the other *Volkdeutsche* – ethnic

Germans – Danny was forced to 'return' to Germany when war broke out. A few years later he would play a key role in my survival, saving my skin at the risk of his own.

I showed some promise on the playing fields. I was fast, strong, and very fit, with the stamina of a regular swimmer, for our home was close enough to the seashore for me to swim every day. But from an early age, my great passion was boxing. My family encouraged my training, for it kept me fit and healthy while my scrapping was, in the main, restricted to the gymnasium, the punch bag and the ring rather than the narrow streets, where pitched battles between Latvian anti-Semites and Jews sometimes occurred.

My boxing was mainly for the well-known Jewish sporting organisation Maccabi, which became a World Union of Jewish athletic clubs in many disciplines in 1921: the same year I was born. Maybe my will to survive was acquired in the ring as I became a boxer, learning to bob, weave and dodge, to feel out an opponent's strengths and weaknesses. Boxing is a martial art that teaches everything from how to stand and breathe in combat to the complex intuition and psychological warfare that decide many matches. It is a full-contact sport, with an arsenal of hooks, jabs, uppercuts, punches that may look simple to spectators, but take years of practice to use effectively. And it was a sport for which I had a natural talent.

I loved practising with heavy bags, circuit training and sparring with my friends as we prepared for competition. We fought in tournaments against other clubs, including an Irish team of friendly rivals that I remember well. We met them four or five times every year, fighting matches of three rounds, each three minutes in duration. As in most amateur boxing, the majority of victories were won on points. Although head guards were not in use back then, we wore thick, heavy gloves that made it difficult to knock out an opponent, even with the strongest of headshots. But that never stopped me from trying.

I was quite highly rated as a boxer, a champion at my weight. I can't remember my exact history in the ring, but I must have won more fights than I lost. I honestly do not recall a single defeat. But life-saving as my training would prove a few years on, at the time it was just a much-loved hobby, and with all that was to follow, the details hardly register in memory now. On weekdays, I was a schoolboy, and I wanted to learn, to advance in my studies as far as I could. However, my education, like that of all ambitious Jewish boys in Riga, was to be cut short.

Although as a child, I knew little of Hitler's rise to power and his growing persecution of the Jews, things in Latvia were also changing rapidly. In 1934, the Free Latvian Republic's nationalist Prime Minister, Kārlis Ulmanis, declared Martial Law, on the pretext that Lieutenant Colonel Voldemārs Ozols, the leader of a small extremist right-wing group, was plotting to overthrow the government. Democracy in Latvia came to an end.

Ulmanis and his government were popular with ethnic Latvians. As dictator, he set about nationalising many industries, with agriculture, manufacturing and the banks all coming under state control. Though he did not round us Jews up in Ghettos or send the army to destroy us, Ulmanis was an anti-Semite, and his promise of 'Latvia for the Latvians' was understood by all to mean the country's wealth would be enjoyed only by his ethnic Latvian followers. As an American diplomat reported to the State Department:

The application of anti-Semitism in Latvia is made very easy by the administrative technique of the country. Nearly everything is permitted but only on the basis of a special permit. If a Jew wishes to establish a business, dismiss or engage employees, move his residence, transfer his business premises, or perform any of the other innumerable functions of life or business, such a permit is usually withheld without explanation. In addition, under the pretext of recruiting additional labour for the land, Jewish households are being deprived of any servant under fifty years of age. There is, moreover, discrimination against Jewish lawyers, doctors and dentists. I am informed in this connection that no Jewish lawyers have been admitted to practise since the coup d'état on 15 May 1934.

There was little opposition to Ulmanis, as much of the country prospered under his rule, even through the worst years of the Great Depression. Those who did resist, mostly communist and Nazi sympathisers, were jailed or killed. When Hitler, upon President Von Hindenburg's death in 1934, abolished the office of President, taking on its powers and declaring himself 'Führer und Reichskanzler', Ulmanis seems to have been watching closely. In 1936, when Latvian President Alberts Kviesis's term of office came to an end, Ulmanis merged the powers of President and Prime Minister, becoming Head of State as well as Head of Government.

Still, to Jews facing the more vicious oppression of Nazi Germany and Stalin's Russia, where hundreds of thousands of Jews had been killed or sent to Siberian labour camps, Latvia seemed a place of relative safety. Many fled to Latvia in the decades between the Wars, in the tragic, false belief that it offered them their best chance of survival.

My father had no such illusions, and knew that war was coming. When Ulmanis first seized power, it was time, he decided, for the family to pack our bags and leave Riga for the Promised Land, to join the Zionist struggle to create a Jewish State.

Zionism is not easy for even Jews to understand – and can mean many things, from the Beitar Zionism of my family to the socialist Zionism of David Ben-Gurion and Golda Meir. These days, it is sometimes assumed that to define onself as a 'Zionist' marks one as a bloodthirsty racist and hater of Palestinians. But Zionism is, very simply, an ideology of survival, born in its modern form in the late eighteenth century, when the secular Jewish journalist Theodor Herzl covered the infamous Dreyfus case. A French-Jewish army officer falsely convicted of treason, Dreyfus convinced Herzl and many other modern European Jews that their hopes of 'assimilation' into Europe's peoples were in vain. Jews, Herzl realised, would never be allowed to assimilate into Europe, and our survival could only be guaranteed by the creation of a Jewish State. The movement grew, despite the early opposition of many Rabbis, who argued that the Jews were condemned to live in exile till the Messiah came. But as anti-Semitism increased across Europe, many Jews became devoted to the Zionist cause, and factions formed within the movement – left, right, and religious. But though these differences could at times lead to violence and great discrimination, all Zionists agreed that only a Jewish State with its own army could bring an end to the massacres and pogroms of European Jewish history.

For a brief while there was hope that we could get away from the Russians and nationalists as we had a relative, uncle Mattison, in Bordeaux, who promised to get us out of Latvia and then, hopefully, on to Palestine. Mattison, my mother's brother, was also from Riga, and had married a French wife. Their son was the same age as me, and we both had our Bar Mitzvah, marking the official end of childhood, in France, when we were thirteen.

Our second trip to France, two years later, began a chain of events that was to change the lives of every member of the Shapov family.

It was a long journey, fraught with danger as we travelled through Warsaw, a brooding Berlin and a frightened Paris before joining my uncle in the French Port of Bordeaux. From there we sailed on a cramped ship to Beirut before the British authorities forced us to turn back. Our papers, they declared, were not in order, and back we went to Riga, crushed by disappointment.

It was a disappointment that my father could not live with. Shortly after our return to Latvia, he decided that he had to try again – and, this time, to try alone. He believed that we would stand a better chance of winning entry as a family if he first made his way to Palestine and settled there, finding work and a home in which we would then join him at the earliest opportunity. Or so he argued, and as a youth, it did not occur to me to question the father who I loved and trusted. But he still lacked the proper visas, and bought passage on a Swedish coal ship, docked in Riga on its way to Palestine. A cargo vessel, it was not meant to carry passengers, and would draw little attention from Passport Control. He could easily blend in with the disembarking crew, and when they left port, a few days later, who would notice that there was one less 'sailor' aboard than when they had arrived?

Perhaps he honestly believed, or convinced himself that he believed, that somehow, despite having smuggled himself into the country, he would soon convince the British not just to grant him right of residence, but to allow his wife and sons to join him. I do not like to think otherwise. He was not a stupid man, and whatever his intentions, the effect was the same. He abandoned us, three young boys and our sick mother, in a Latvia that was becoming more and more unfriendly to the Jews.

My youth came to an end with his departure. At fourteen, I was now head of the family, charged with caring for my lonely, unwell mother, and supporting my two brothers. With little choice, I left school and went to work. I took a job packing boxes in a warehouse and chopped meat for a local butcher to supplement my meagre wages. Childhood was a prized memory, but as for youth, it passed me by, without my even realising it was gone. I had other things on my mind.

Even when my father had been at his most successful, we were never more than comfortable, financially – after he left, we became a poor family indeed. I worked all the hours that I could, but we considered ourselves lucky when lunch consisted of a sandwich. We were happy enough to have a piece of bread. We heard nothing from Dad: he was supposed to be in

Palestine, preparing our new home, but the mail was unreliable, and no telegrams arrived.

It was all that I could do to earn enough to feed the family, while we waited for his call to come and join him in the Holy Land. When I found time, I continued with my boxing, mostly in Beitar, which had established an organisation, almost a kind of commune, providing help to Jewish families that had lost a parent. I made many friends amongst my comrades in the movement, learning to use weapons and the arts of warfare, lessons that would prove invaluable in years to come. I would also pay a price for this allegiance, as the followers of Beitar were hated by the left-wing Zionists, who called us 'Jewish fascists' and treated us like dirt. Much as I enjoyed my training and social life in Beitar, I had little free time for such pursuits. The priority was to keep my family alive and fed. We lived in hope of escape – but as the years passed, hope was fading.

Finally, in 1939, a message reached the family from Palestine. Dad told us to sell the house and everything we could, pack up and join him in the Promised Land. We were all thrilled at the prospect of being reunited as a family. It took months to sell the house and save enough to buy the necessary documents and tickets, and it was almost a year later when we set out, once again, on what we thought would be a great adventure.

Dad had given me the name of an agent, a friend of his from Riga, who helped us to arrange our papers and book passage to Syria, this time via Bucharest, the Romanian capital.

After many months of hard work, both in and out of the warehouse, the deal was done. The agent presented us with our travel documents and tickets. He also expressed concern, for we were planning to travel with a large amount of cash, everything we'd raised. It would be safer, he suggested, if we instead took a cheque that we could cash in Bucharest, before sailing on to Palestine: a cheque he could provide us with, of course.

He was very persuasive and a friend of my father's – his arguments seemed prudent, and we trusted the man. We gave him almost all our money for that small piece of paper, saving just a few notes for the trip. I even remember thanking him for all his help and generosity as we waved farewell.

But when, with several other families, we arrived in Bucharest, we learned we had been duped. Our 'generous' agent was not the friend that we had thought – his cheque bounced, and our documents were fakes. At least, we thought, we had our tickets for the crossing, but when we presented them at the docks we found we had been cheated yet again. Three of our four tickets were forgeries, absolutely useless. My mother collapsed on the spot in a dead faint when she realised a family friend had robbed us and she was not, after all, going to join her husband.

The agent had deceived and cheated the Shapov

family at our most vulnerable, taken our money and, we discovered on our return to Riga, bought himself a safe and luxurious passage to Israel where he would live as a rich man. I never forgot his name or face and would have killed him at the time, if I'd been able to lay hands on him. Many years later, I bumped into him by accident in Israel and my anger, which had never left me, boiled over. I gave him the beating he deserved but spared his life.

When my mother was revived, there at the dock-side, she insisted that I use the one good ticket to join my beloved father in Palestine. But how could I leave a woman who had already undergone heart surgery twice to look after a boy of twelve and another of seven? I simply could not abandon her. Who cared about one ticket? We would leave either as a family, this time, or not at all.

We were in Bucharest for a few short days before deciding we had no choice but to return to Riga. We had virtually no money left at all, and could not afford to eat, let alone try and find another route to join my father. What did we know of life outside of Riga? I didn't even think to try and sell our one valid ticket. Getting home from Bucharest was complicated, and we changed from train to train until at last we found ourselves in a stalled locomotive on the Russian border, as fighter planes flew overhead. We took cover as best we could in ditches till the bombers had passed, and finally made it back to Riga.

With the house sold, we took a small apartment in Maskavas, a suburb mostly occupied by poor Latvians, Russians and Jews. It was all we could afford, and then only with assistance from Beitar. The war had come to Latvia, and our failure to escape would tear the family apart. We did not know it at the time, and the full story would not come to light until 1945, but the Baltic states were to be a crucial battleground in the years of war ahead.

CHAPTER THREE

THE SOVIET OCCUPATION

In 1939, the world had been caught off guard when Hitler's 'anti-Bolshevik' regime, which had always condemned the Soviets as Jewish Pawns in propaganda, signed a 'non-aggression pact' with Stalin, the Molotov-Ribbentrop agreement. Officially, the treaty pledged that the two countries would stay neutral in the event of either going to war with a third country: in fact, it was the document which not only began the war, but decided the terrible fate that Latvia and her Baltic neighbours would suffer in the years to come.

A secret protocol appended to the treaty divided Northern and Eastern Europe into Nazi and Stalinist 'spheres of influence', with the two regimes agreeing to divide Poland, while Latvia, Finland, the other Baltic states and parts of Romania and Hungary were allocated to the 'Soviet Sphere'. This agreement also led to a vast increase in trade between the two dicta-torships. The Germans lacked raw materials, from oil and the rubber crucial for an army's boots and tyres, to the metals needed to build tanks. Once war began, the Allied trade blockade on Germany would leave Hitler's army helpless – unless an agreement could be reached with the Soviets. Russia's vast mineral wealth and access to trade routes into Asia overcame Hitler's distaste for communism. Russian raw materials were exchanged for German armaments and planes. Of course, the two empires would soon use the very goods they had exchanged against each other.

In 1939, Stalin had negotiated on two fronts, enter-ing military pacts with first the Allies – and then Germany, even going so far as to propose Soviet membership of the Axis. The war began with Hitler's invasion of Poland – an invasion that Stalin's armies joined, the two countries dividing the conquered nation between them, and even holding joint victory parades. Under the terms of the pact, 1939 also saw the repatriation of over 50,000 ethnic Germans from Latvia to the Reich, amongst them my friend Danny. Ulmanis was forced to grant the Soviets the right to garrison 30,000 Russian troops in Latvia, as well as building special airfields for Soviet use and handing over three military bases. Perhaps he hoped to forestall an invasion, and for a while, as the Red Army strug-gled to take Finland, it seemed that Stalin's meddling in Latvia's affairs would end there.

The summer of 1940 finished all such hopes. With the international community's attention on the Western Front, as Germany invaded France, the Russians took the Baltic states in a few short weeks. To conceal their naked imperialism, the Soviets engineered mass protests against Ulmanis, though the 'protestors', demanding that Latvia join the Soviet Union, were in fact Russian agents. The Soviets called for an 'election' in July 1940, to decide the country's fate. Latvia's political parties formed a National Committee, to unite against the Soviets: the Russians promptly banned the committee and arrested its members. Only the communist 'Latvian People's Working Bloc' was allowed to appear on the ballot paper.

Unsurprisingly, the Latvian People's Working Bloc won by a landslide, in what the Soviets claimed was a staggering 97 per cent turnout. Why bother voting in an election that can have only one outcome? The Russians provided an excellent reason. Failure to vote was 'treachery against the people', a crime punishable by death. To make the whole obscene charade yet more absurd, the exact result was announced in Moscow – twelve hours before the polls had closed.

This sick joke of a Parliament convened a few days later, and voted unanimously to 'apply' to join the Soviet Union, as did similar puppet assemblies in Lithuania and Estonia. The Russians graciously accepted these petitions, and Latvia became the fifteenth Republic of

the USSR. Already, tens of thousands had died fighting the invasion, and the Soviets were quick to impose
their usual harsh regime.

Ulmanis gave a final radio address, pleading with
the Latvian people not to resist the occupation,
knowing full well that Stalin would put down any
uprising with merciless force. 'I will remain in my
place and you must remain in your places,' he told his
people. Those words may have saved lives, preventing
his loyal followers from forming a resistance movement, but they were far from true. The Soviets forced
his resignation, and deported him to Stavropol. They
jailed him one year later, and he died of dysentery
in 1942, while being transported to a new prison in
Turkmenistan. A lifetime later, his great-nephew,
Gustav Ulmanis, became the first elected President of
a newly-independent Latvia.

But in 1940, the Soviets set about destroying
Latvian nationalism, imprisoning hundreds of men
and women who had worked for the Ulmanis government, and nationalising the country's land by decree.
Latvian diplomats were given twenty-four hours
to recognise the new Soviet-installed government:
those who declined forfeited their property and were
sentenced to death. Soon, it was declared a capital
offence to be related to anyone in hiding from the
government, or those who tried to flee.

Russian rule had always been harsh on Latvia's
Jewish population, and most Latvian Jews felt much

the same as their Christian neighbours where the Russians were concerned. Over the centuries, Tsarist regimes had variously ordered the expulsion of all Jews, levied harsh taxes and special restrictions on those few Jews it granted right of residence, and lagged a century behind Western Europe when it came to the emancipation of Jews. But the 'ethnic' Latvians had known centuries of German domination before the Russians came, and though early German settlers had terrorised the native Balts, forcing their conversion to Christianity from native paganism, that had been largely forgotten in the intervening centuries. Thus Latvian nationalists, though influenced by successive occupying cultures, including, at times, those of Polish and Swedish rule, felt a strong sense of kinship with the German people, a kinship Latvia's Jews, including those with roots in Germany, did not share.

Although thousands of Jews had fought and died for Latvia's independence, and thousands more would be deported to Siberia in the brief Soviet Occupation before the Nazis came, Latvian Jews were always viewed with some suspicion by most Latvians. The Nazi claim, made in Hitler's *Mein Kampf*, but echoed in much German writing of the time, that the Soviets were 'Bolshevik Pawns' of the 'international Jewish conspiracy', was swallowed wholesale by many Latvians. Jews were widely believed to be communist and pro-Russian: ironically, in part because many Jews did flee from Russia to Latvia, to escape Stalinist oppression. Thus the Russian massacres of Latvians (some of them Jewish) in 1905 were blamed by some Latvian nationalists on the Jews. Just as Hitler's anti-communism won him support, before the war, from some British and American politicians, so many Latvians, including the educated, began to equate all Jews with communism and then Stalinism.

This was ridiculous, of course. As the saying has it, put three Jews on a desert island and you end up with three synagogues, two political parties and an entryist faction that tries to infiltrate them both. There were Jewish communists, including some who played a role in the Russian revolution: but there were also Jewish conservatives, secular Jewish liberals and religious factions of both left and right. My family's politics, though we did not often speak of them, were of the Jewish Right and its influential leader, Vladimir Ze'ev Jabotinsky. We were not just anti-communists: even fellow Zionists of the left-wing type despised us. But the reality made no difference – we were Jews, so we were suspects to many of our fellow Latvian citizens, secret allies, if not puppet-masters, of the Soviets.

These prejudices were not held by all non-Jewish Latvians, of course, and in the early years of the Free Latvian Republic, with the hated Russian occupiers gone, we enjoyed more freedom and safety than Jews across much of Europe. But in the background, even amongst some of those we thought of as our friends and neighbours, the old suspicion lurked – and in time, would see Latvia and the other Baltic states face some of the worst brutality of the Holocaust.

Some Jews believed at first the Russians might at least protect us from the Germans, but this was desperately naive. Stalin had purged his Foreign Ministry of Jews to curry favour with the Nazis prior to the Molotov-Ribbentrop negotiations, while the Soviets were secretly negotiating to join the Axis powers in 1939 and 1940, and had no intention of showing mercy to any Baltic citizens, Gentile or Jew.

The Russian occupation at first had little direct impact on my life. I had Russian friends in Riga, as I do now in the United States, and while I had no great love for the Russian Empire or its communist successor, given their oppression of the Jews, my family was not targeted for deportation by the Russians. We had no property to 'nationalise', in our small rented apartment, and though I was a sworn anti-communist, I did not advertise the fact. The Soviet occupiers were mostly concerned with Latvians they thought 'a counter-revolutionary' threat – those loyal to Ulmanis, and his nationalists, and I continued to work, supporting my family.

One day, I returned to our apartment, in the Maskavas suburb, to find my mother in tears. The Russians had drafted Boris into the Red Army, and we knew only that he was in transit to the USSR, for training. We never heard from him again, and it was only much, much later that I learned he had survived the war. Where we had been, just years before, a happy, normal family, with a mother, father and three brothers, living comfortably enough, now only three of us remained – my ailing mother, little Fima and myself – with food scarce and me struggling to support my family as best I could, in the small apartment in Maskavas. It was a terrible moment for us all, and my heart was full of hatred for the Russians and their part in decimating my family still further.

On 13 and 14 June 1941, the Soviets began a programme of mass deportations. Under the detailed Serov instructions, some 35,000 Latvians, including thousands of Jews, were woken from their beds, and given one hour to pack a few possessions – clothing, a little money, and kitchen utensils – before being taken to the nearest railway station. Only then were the men separated from their wives and children, families torn apart without warning. The deportees were herded into cattle trucks, without toilets, and the trains left for Siberia. The men – identified as 'anti-Soviet elements' – were sent to Gulag labour camps, while their families were imprisoned in the many forced resettlement zones in remote parts of the Soviet Union. Almost 2 per cent of Latvia's whole population had been swallowed by the Russians in a few short nights: but more of them would return, in time, than ever came back from the German concentration camps.

The Nazi-Soviet alliance soon came to an end. Hitler had not welcomed the Soviet interpretation of the pact, with the Russians giving no advance warning before invading Lithuania. As the Russians annexed the three Baltic states, Hitler began to fear that they were building an anti-German bloc. Disputes over the borders of Hungary and Romania added to the tension, and although these were resolved, Hitler's belief that war with Russia was 'inevitable' began to reassert itself. Planning for the invasion began in 1940.

Historians now argue that it was Hitler's opening up an Eastern front that led, in time, to the Allied triumph in the war. Convinced that the Slavs were inferior to his 'Aryan Race' and unimpressed by the Red Army's performance in the Finnish war of 1939-40, it is said that Hitler expected a quick and easy victory, winning Russia's oil for the Reich – and a vast supply of slave labour. He apparently believed the stubborn British would soon beg for peace once the Swastika was raised above the Kremlin, and that the Nazis had the advantage of surprise – after all, the Soviets formed a neutrality pact with both the Reich and its Japanese ally, and had sought membership of the Axis.

But while Stalin was slow to recognise the German threat, by May of 1940 he was speaking, too, of the inevitability of war: it was difficult to overlook the German build-up, what with millions of German troops massing on the Soviet border. Yet he failed to mobilise his forces, perhaps finding it impossible to quite believe that the Germans would attack so soon after the joint invasion of Poland, and believing they would first prosecute the war with Britain to a victorious conclusion before challenging Mother Russia. Whatever the reasons, the pact came to a violent end just weeks after the deportations, in the early hours of 21 June 1941.

Hitler had believed that the Russians could not afford to leave the Baltic states – but after several catastrophic losses, the Red Army turned and fled, under aerial bombardment from the Luftwaffe. The Germans entered Latvia through Lithuania, with many Lithuanian Jews fleeing from their advance, and the murder of Jews began at once.

The invading armies had been sent into the Baltics with a new strategy to address the 'Jewish problem', as the Nazis called it. Whereas in Poland they had built Ghettos, intended to operate as long-term prisons, and subjected Jews in Germany to humiliating restrictions under the Nuremberg Laws, it was in the Baltic states that the Holocaust truly began. The SS came in with orders to immediately set about murdering Baltic Jews – and they enlisted the assistance of many Latvians. Furious at the oppression they had faced under the Soviets, even Latvians who had been our friends and neighbours were quick to blame the 'Bolshevik' Jews for the loss of their families and friends, and the SS skilfully exploited Latvian anti-Semitism, recruiting Latvian Militias to join their murderous campaign. Nothing we had faced under Ulmanis or the Russians could have prepared us for what came as the German Armies approached Riga, welcomed by the Latvians as 'liberators' from Russian Rule.

The Soviets had taken Boris; the Nazis and their Latvian allies would do much, much worse.

CHAPTER FOUR

THE RIGA GHETTO

In the final days of June 1941, every Jew in Riga could hear the marching jackboots as the Germans drove towards the city, and stories of atrocities reached us with the arrival of refugees from across Latvia. Our Latvian 'neighbours' were quick to turn on us. We heard that Christian Latvians had pointed Jews out to the invaders – in towns like Asīte, Priekule, Grobina and Durbe, Jews were massacred first by Germans, and then by the Latvian collaborators who joined the SS. Their units, known as the 'Latvian Auxiliary Police', were under the command of the SS Einsatzgruppen – death squads, formed by SS-Obergruppenführer Reinhard Heydrich – and would in time kill as many Jews in Latvia as the Germans themselves. The campaign to exterminate the Jews was named in 'honour' of this SS Leader: Operation Reinhard, and in Latvia, it came close to success.

Thousands died in that first week, before the Germans took Riga. On 29 June, in the town of Jelgava, the first unit of Latvian Irregulars under direct German command was formed. Mārtiņš Vagulāns, a former member of the Pērkonkrusts, a fascist party that had been banned under Ulmanis, was appointed leader of 300 Latvian murderers, supervised by officers of the SS, including Rudolf Batz, who later became head of the Gestapo in Hanover.

Over the summer of 1941, Batz and his men delighted their German overseers, killing 2,000 Jews in Jelgava and the surrounding region of Zemgale. The historic Jelgava Synagogue was burned down on 4 July, by the combined efforts of Batz's men and Einsatzgruppe A.

After days of artillery bombardment, Riga was quiet on the night on 30 June – and then, that morning, the radio, which had been silent for weeks, suddenly broadcast the Latvian National Anthem, followed by the Nazi Horst Wessel song. The Germans took Riga on 1 July. The young Viktors Arājs, inspired by Batz and the Pērkonkrusts' call for 'patriotic' Latvians to join the SS as they swept through Latvia killing Jews, contacted Walter Stahlecker, SS-Brigadeführer and Generalmajor der Polizei, commander of SS Einsatzgruppe A.

Stahlecker must have been impressed with Arājs, sensing his psychopathic potential and leadership qualities, for he granted him permission to form his own Kommando unit and begin immediate pogroms.

Hundreds of Latvian students in right-wing fraternities joined with Arājs – though Pērkonkrusts had been suppressed, first by Ulmanis and then the Soviets, they had many imitators, and it was not difficult to recruit would-be killers ... and some with experience. The Nazi sympathisers who had been imprisoned by Ulmanis were released by the Gestapo, and found employment in the new Auxiliary 'Police Forces' – paramilitary collaborators.

Arājs Kommando began operations on the night of 3 July. Jews were beaten, robbed, and killed, arrested and turned over to the Gestapo. The very next night and day saw Jews across Riga, including refugees from Lithuania, rounded up and forced into the city's synagogues in Maskavas, Gogol Street and Stabu Street before the buildings were burned to the ground, killing hundreds. The Stabu Street Synagogue massacre was led by aviator Herberts Cukurs, the 'Butcher of Riga', who dragged Jews inside, locked the doors and set the building alight. Eyewitness accounts tell of the dying, of their screams, of Jews in flames breaking through the windows from inside and trying to escape. Cukurs shot them. The Biķernieku forest became a killing field, with 4,000 Riga Jews murdered there in July, mostly by the Latvian irregulars.

Those of us who survived the first wave of massacres were soon imprisoned in the Ghetto, set up in the very suburb in which I had grown up. The neighbourhood was surrounded with barbed wire by the Germans and their Latvian allies, and we were instructed that this was where we were to live, sleep and eat. We would, they told us, be picked up every morning and sent on work details. Of course, this applied only to the strong and fit young men. Women, invalids and children were a different story. To the occupiers, they were an unwanted burden, taking up valuable space and eating food needed for the troops, Kapos, and slave labourers. The Nazis and their Latvian allies simply disposed of them.

It still makes me weep to recall how low the Germans and some amongst the Latvians had sunk. First they took out all the elderly Jews, humiliated them as they made them shed their clothes (these, unbelievably, were washed and sent back to Berlin), lined them up on the edge of a huge pit in the Earth and opened fire with machine guns, sending them tumbling into a mass grave. The women and children then faced the same treatment, their bodies dancing madly as the bullets flew.

These were actions of men who called themselves 'soldiers', massacring the old, the infirm, women and small children, none of whom could fight back in any way. They could not even die with dignity, their very clothing taken from them. My heart was heavy and I feared desperately for my mother and young brother Ephraim. I was determined to find them within the segregated Ghetto, and save them if I could.

As the occupying forces marched their helpless prisoners through the streets I stood on the sidewalk and scanned every face, desperately hoping to see Fima in the crowds. But he never appeared. One day, I spotted a Jewish girl I used to go out with, with her little brother Osha bringing up the rear of a group of captives. On the spur of the moment I decided that if I could not find my own brother I should help someone else. My heart thumping, I approached one of the Latvian traitors, pointed out the boy, said that he was my brother and asked the Latvian to bring him to me. It would have been impossible to rescue Osha's sister and even trying would have drawn murderous attention. She pushed Osha towards me and with tears running down her face went to what she knew was her death.

The Latvian I approached looked me up and down when I made my request as though I was something he had picked up on his shoe and told me I was crazy. His attitude changed when I offered him one of my precious gold roubles. With a sly look over his shoulder, the Latvian stepped into the crowd of Jews, grabbed the boy and gave him to me, pocketing his 'reward' and striding off to rejoin his newfound friends.

Osha remained with me right through the ordeal until we were liberated four years later. Four years! It doesn't sound long in the ordinary run of things, does it? Yet it was a lifetime.

Some while later I managed to slip out of the Ghetto after work in another bid to try and find what was left of my family. I made my way carefully to the house in Maskavas where we had lived together before the Germans marched into town, avoiding all contact like a thief in the night. But when I arrived the apartment was empty and there was blood on the floor. I instantly realised what had happened. They had been taken. Alive or dead I did not know.

There was a bottle of vodka hidden in the kitchen. Overwhelmed with shock and horror, I drank it in gulps, crying as I swallowed. Before I knew it, the bottle was empty, though it could barely numb my pain. I passed out in the kitchen and slept for two whole days, less from the alcohol, I think, than to keep myself from thinking of what had happened to my family.

When I recovered I staggered to my feet and went in search of neighbours. I asked what had happened and my worst fears were realised. They had been taken by the Germans. I could see others being shepherded away to be taken into a camp but I was helpless. I wanted to scream and shout, to fight everyone who was doing this to my beloved family but I could do nothing because of the barbed wire and the fact that the feared and heavily armed SS surrounded us.

I later learned that my precious mother had died of a heart attack and I could only assume that the worst had happened to my brother. It was the natural assumption to make, for the massacres and random killings continued through the summer. Construction of the Ghetto had begun in late July, with 20,000 Latvians and 12,000 Russians moved out of the Maskavas area. On 25 October 1941, an official order was given that all Jews in Riga were to move into the Ghetto. Notices appeared around the city, reading: 'All Jews living within the boundaries of Riga City who as yet have not moved to the Ghetto must do so before 25 October at 6 p.m. Those who do not observe this directive will be most severely punished.'

The punishment could not have been worse than that already faced by most of Latvia's Jews, as the SS and Latvian police drove Jewish families from their homes and into the forests, where they were murdered. We had already been subjected to the usual humiliations that the Nazis inflicted upon Jews in conquered nations – forced to wear the Star of David, forbidden to walk in the streets or ride street cars, made to walk in gutters like dogs.

Those of us who lived in Maskavas already were not permitted to stay in our homes, once the barbed wire was erected but were told to find our own accommodation amongst the empty houses. We were allowed to take very little into the Ghetto, just a few items of personal clothing and furniture. The rest of our possessions were seized by the Gestapo and sent back to Germany, though many Latvian Police stole what they could, and the Germans overlooked small thefts, as a 'reward' for joining them in killing Jews. Some historians have argued that the SS and SD (the SS's intelligence agency) were more interested in massacring Jews than taking their property, while the Latvians and German 'civilian administration' were mostly concerned with enriching themselves. Whatever was not scooped up by the Latvians or German soldiers was sent back by the trainload to Berlin – jewellery and other valuables in particular.

☞

By the end of October, 15,000 Jews had already been killed, and the Ghetto was overcrowded with the remnants of the population. There were around 30,000 people squeezed into an area of sixteen blocks, which had originally housed a mere 13,000. The inhabitants, conscious of the coming winter, set up a hospital, schools and soup kitchens, and although the Nazis had at first allowed the Ghetto authorities to make such provisions, their orders were changing rapidly. In September, Hitler had decreed that all German Jews would be deported to the Baltics, meaning the over-crowding would grow worse – and scarce resources would not be put aside for Latvian Jews.

On 27 November, the 'Small Ghetto' was formed – a four-block area within the barbed wire enclosure of the Grosse Ghetto, and able-bodied men were ordered to move to this new Ghetto the next day. The remainder of the population were ordered to report on 30 November for 'light work duties', carrying with them bags of no more than 20 kilograms in weight: a sham, to prevent them realising what lay in store. We feared the worst: the initial massacres had been mostly of able-bodied men, and it seemed that the Small Ghetto was a rounding-up area for those intended to die next.

In fact, orders had been given for the young and strong to be preserved as slave labourers. Roughly 4,000 Jews were separated and confined in the Small Ghetto, while the remainder were rounded up and slaughtered. Whether the massacres were intended simply to meet Hitler's quota of destruction or to make room in the Grosse Ghetto for the arrival of German Jews diverted from Minsk has never been entirely clear. Either way, the forest killings opened up most of the Ghetto for Jews brought in from Germany.

The murders were carried out by the SS Einsatzgruppen and their Latvian Allies, especially the Arājs Kommando unit. Within the Ghetto, the German and Latvian soldiers, many of them drunk, forced families from their homes, shooting wildly to terrorise them. Children were thrown from third-floor windows, and despite the hopeless situation, some Jews attempted to resist – perhaps 1,000 were shot as they were rounded up. At 6 a.m., having been told to 'prepare for a long journey', 15,000 Latvian Jews were marched 10 kilometres to the forest of Rumbula, where Russian POWs had dug mass graves. Their few belongings were taken, and then, once they had been stripped of all their clothes, the 15,000 were machine-gunned to death.

The first trainload of German Jews had arrived from Berlin that morning, but with the Ghetto over-crowded, they were sent directly from the railway station to the nearby forest, and gunned down before the first Latvian prisoners arrived. Himmler then gave orders that no German Jews were to be executed without his authorisation, perhaps from fear of drawing the US into the war.

Room was made for German deportees with further massacres. Another 12,000 were marched out of the Ghetto on 8 December and again murdered naked in the woods. The next day, while those of us still alive were on work detail, the SS and Arājs Kommando searched the Small Ghetto for survivors in hiding, for a small number of people had managed to escape the massacres of the past weeks. Another 500 were taken from the Ghetto to the Biķernieku forest and shot, adding to the 4,000 already buried in the woods' mass graves. Of the 60,000 in Latvia when the Germans invaded, more than half had already been slaughtered.

By December 1942, there were fewer than 5,000 of us left. Across the Baltic states, according to

Himmler's own reports, the six months following the invasion saw the Nazis and their allies murder 136,242 Jews, 10,064 communists, 653 deemed mentally ill, 44 Poles, 5 Gypsies, and one unlucky Armenian. Little is known of the exact numbers of Romany Gypsies murdered in Latvia, but as another 'degenerate species' of *Untermenschen* in Nazi ideology, their whole population was a specific Einsatzgruppen target, and it is estimated that half the Latvian Roma population were exterminated in the war. It should never be forgotten that the Gypsies, still oppressed in much of Europe, though always few in number, were victims of the Holocaust as well. Across Europe, roughly half a million were murdered in the war.

It is hard to say who were the most enthusiastic of our would-be exterminators, between the Einsatzgruppen, the Arājs Kommando, the regular German army and the Kapos in the camps. But the massacres of 1941 were the work of the collaborator forces of Arājs and Cukurs every bit as much as of the Germans. Herberts Cukurs, second in command of the Arāji units, was present at the murders of 30 November, barking orders to his army of murderers and thugs. Some survivors claim that Cukurs, under SS Supervision, was in command of the operation, and he was charged in absentia during the Nuremberg trials, with responsibility for 35,000 deaths. No wonder some called him 'The Butcher of Riga' though there were other contenders for that title. On 30 November, Cukurs fired shots into the Jews massing for transfer to the Ghetto, killing at random. Like many in the Arājs units, he seems to have enjoyed the act of murder.

Cukurs deserves special attention, as perhaps the most brutal of Latvian war criminals. Though charged at Nuremberg, he was not under arrest, and evaded punishment for many years. He escaped to Germany with fleeing German troops in 1944, and promptly vanished, making his way first to France, then to the large community of Nazi criminals in South America. Whether from arrogance or simple stupidity, Cukurs did not even try to hide his identity, living under his own name and working as a pilot in Sao Paulo, flying small groups of tourists over the Brazilian coast. The Israeli authorities informed the Brazilian government of Cukurs' presence and location, but no action was taken, and he remained a free man.

Finally, in 1965, he was lured to a remote house in the city of Montevideo, Uruguay. He had travelled there to discuss setting up an aviation business, but on arrival at the house, found not investors but a group of Mossad agents. There was a brief struggle, and Cukurs, who had murdered so many with his own hands, given orders for the execution of thousands more, was shot. Soon after, a message was sent to newspapers in South America and Germany, reading:

Taking into consideration the gravity of the charge
levelled against the accused, namely that he personally supervised the killing of more than 30,000 men,
women and children, and considering the extreme
display of cruelty which the subject showed when
carrying out his tasks, the accused Herberts Cukurs
is hereby sentenced to death. Accused was executed
by those who can never forget on the 23 February
1965. His body can be found at Casa Cubertini Calle
Colombia, Séptima Sección del Departamento de
Canelones, Montevideo, Uruguay.

The Police investigated and found Cukurs' body. It
cannot be said that Justice had been done – Cukurs
could never have faced a punishment compara-
ble to his crimes – but at least he would not draw
another breath.

Incredibly, however, recent years have seen
attempts, in Latvia, to rehabilitate the memory
of Cukurs. This is one of many reasons I can never
return to Latvia: the hatred of Jews remains strong
amongst much of the local population, and though
a memorial in Biķernieku Forest acknowledges the
part played by Latvian collaborators in the Holocaust,
many nationalists continue to deny or minimise the
atrocities committed by 'Patriots' such as Cukurs.
In 2004, incredibly, commemorative envelopes were
issued, dedicated to Cukurs! The Latvian Foreign
Minister condemned the envelopes, acknowledging

that Cukurs was a War Criminal, who played a key part in the destruction of Latvia's Jews. But his words were chosen carefully – those who had issued the envelopes, he said, 'did not understand' the reality of Latvia's history in the Second World War. I suspect they understood, all too well, and that it was Cukurs' brutality that the Neo-Nazi nationalist scum had set out to commemorate. There have even been petitions to the prosecutor's office, pleading Cukurs be exonerated. Though these were rejected, the very fact that they were issued in the first place shows how little some Latvian 'nationalism' has changed.

CHAPTER FIVE

DUCKING, BOBBING AND WEAVING

A good boxer never gets caught on his heels. He ducks, he bobs, he weaves, he stays out of his opponent's reach. Those were the rules I lived by, outside of the ring as well. My secret was to keep fit and strong, so that I was always looked upon as 'useful' by our oppressors, while ignoring as many of the rules and regulations, especially over food and clothing, as I could without being executed. I kept out of the way of the Kapos and the SS as much as possible.

Gradually we settled into a nightmarish life in our little Ghetto. The quaint old stone and wooden buildings, so attractive in my childhood, had become a grey, brooding prison, lacking only bars on the windows. Our little group, the Strong Ones, were always on the lookout for anything useful, especially food to keep us alive and alcohol, both to drink, but, more importantly, to barter.

We had been careful to pick a house in the Maskavas Forštate with a cellar that, by the strategic placement of a big, heavy wooden cupboard, we were able to disguise; it completely covered the entrance to our Aladdin's Cave. This was our basement where we kept the wine, the vodka, conserves and other luxuries not to mention the gun and ammunition I had acquired. A lot of the contents we obtained from the town, exchanging items which had been left behind when families were moved out on a minutes' notice and overlooked by the German scavengers.

Few inmates knew about our cellar, no more than half a dozen, and we had to keep it that way, otherwise there was always a chance of being sold out by a jealous outsider or even one of our own, under Gestapo interrogation. The cellar was not only our store but our refuge as well. When we wanted to vanish for a while we would disappear down to the basement. No one knew where we were and I would often spend a couple of days down there with my thoughts and a drink. For all the Germans and Latvians knew, I was at the bottom of a grave or simply out on a work party. They didn't ask and I didn't tell.

Some sort of escape was needed after the massacres in Rumbula and Biķernieku Forests took place and the vodka dulled the memory for a short time as the Germans took out Jewish families as they sat eating at their tables and replaced them with others, mostly German Jews. Sometimes they would come in and would even finish the meals left half-eaten on the tables. It sounds amoral but we all took food when it was available.

Who were the lucky ones: those who were put to death in the gas chambers or shot, or those who were sent to live a life of misery in the camps? Death was not an option as far as I was concerned, living was far too important and I felt that our time would come one day.

Everyone who came into our extended Ghetto had a different story according to where they came from, Germany, Czechoslovakia, Austria and other points from around Europe. There were lurid tales of extreme cruelty, of forced abortions, the battering of little children, Jews buried alive with those who had been gassed or shot. All the tales were truly terrible but, sadly, easy to believe.

The Germans under Hitler were self-styled Gods. They could walk into any house, and country, and take what they wanted, killing as they went. If I live to be a hundred – and I am well on the way – I will never forgive or forget. I still feel so bitter I will not ride in a German car. How could I forget?

In the Riga Ghetto it was a constant battle for food, for dignity and, most of all, survival. Every day we were called to duty, to work on the railway, in the warehouse, on the roads or in the Ghetto. We were always dreading the call to cemetery duty, the one-way ticket to eternity after digging your own grave.

Whenever I could, I would engineer my way to warehouse duty, for that offered the best opportunity to steal food and fill my belly, essential in the battle for survival. I hunted everywhere for something to eat, and learned my way around the warehouse and the German army quartermaster stores, where they shipped in all the provisions to feed their troops. Of course, it was we Strong Ones who unloaded the supply trains as they brought in perishables, wine, and other rations. I knew exactly where to find everything, and took whatever I could. The punishment for being caught was usually death … but then that applied to most things that displeased our 'masters'.

I became an expert thief. I even made myself a big 'Shylock' coat like pickpockets in the movies. I removed the lining and was left with a perfect poaching sack which allowed me to liberate enough food not only to keep myself alive, but also to help those less fortunate than me and unable to fend for themselves.

Fortunately I had an arrangement with my old friend Herr Rudy Harr. An ex-boxer himself, he was now in his late forties, a member of the Ghetto Police, and a decent man. In return for his turning his back on my pilfering, I split all my loot with him, 50/50.

Of course it was a risky business for both of us, because with so much valuable food and drink in the vicinity the place swarmed with soldiers, and sometimes the SS as well. Harr had a bad reputation amongst my fellow prisoners who claimed he was a double agent, spying on the Ghetto population and turning his own German Jews over to the SS. I have never been able to believe this – he could have had me killed time and time again, but in fact saved my life.

Inevitably it was an SS man who eventually worked out that this tubby little Jew in front of him was considerably bulkier than he should have been for someone on a starvation diet. He eyed me with some distaste as I kept my head lowered to the ground and my eyes averted from him. It was not enough as he growled at me to stop where I was. He yanked open my coat and discovered the salami, whisky and other luxuries I had taken that day. There was no chance of escape as he quickly summoned his fellow Nazis.

They spat at me, calling me a stinking Jew and much worse. I was knocked from my feet and kicked there on the ground, their jackboots hurting far more than their insults as my kidneys took a pounding. I was terrified, white and shaking with fear, for it seemed this beating would inevitably end in execution. Only a couple of days before, I had watched them hang a couple of my comrades in public for stealing a few grams of rancid butter, an example to all of us, they said, and here was I with a shop full of groceries in comparison.

I couldn't even go down fighting as I had always promised myself I would if the end came. At last, they tired of beating me, but there was no sign of reprieve. They dragged me to their headquarters where my friend Harr was ordered to shave off my hair, another ominous sign. They often shaved the heads of prisoners before execution.

Incredibly, though, they did not kill me there and then, instead throwing me into a basement where I was left to rot with a dozen or more other hapless Jews, none of whom had committed crimes as serious as mine. Our diet in that stinking hole was just mildewed bread and stale water. I guess they saw that as a fitting part of my punishment.

My only hope was Harr and when I was finally dragged out to face the music he was standing alongside the senior SS man, Obersturmführer Szlamek Zauer, looking at me with his cold eyes. He asked who had given me the food and I answered that I had taken it myself because I was hungry.

Harr then said: 'Is that the last time you are going to do that sort of thing?'

Surprised, I quickly answered 'Yes', waiting with trepidation for what seemed certain to follow. It was definitely my last time if they were going to execute me!

Sure enough my stomach turned to liquid when the SS man unfastened his holster, took out his pistol and said: 'Next time you are seen doing anything like this again I will shoot you myself. If it wasn't for this man Harr supporting you, you would be dead right now. I won't hang you because that would be too good for you. You have been stealing our soldiers' food out of their mouths to eat for yourself and to give to other stinking Jews. This is the last time.'

He kicked my backside, hard, and told me to get back to work. I could not believe what was happening. Harr had somehow managed to talk him out of it, not solely because he was an accomplice and a friend but because of our old friendship, forged in the gymnasiums where we'd both learned to love boxing. I am sure that played a huge part in my unexpected reprieve.

Despite being weak and tired I was back unloading the train the next day – and still stealing food. It proved that we all looked the same to the Germans for, having caught me so well-stocked, it would have been logical to keep an especially close eye on me.

Why would I take such a risk when my very life was hanging by a thread? I was hungry and nothing is stronger in life than hunger, especially when there is food within reach. I would do anything for an extra piece of bread. Harr, too, continued to receive his share of my spoils despite the risk to himself. The only care I took was not to overload my coat pockets with too much again.

Our ration was 250 grams of bread for twenty-four hours and some warm water they called 'pea soup' but which smelled and tasted much like dishwater, with a similar consistency. There was no water in which to wash, only enough for an occasional cup of strange tasting 'coffee' probably made out of acorns.

But for me cleanliness was dignity, an essential part of maintaining my pride and will to live. When I finished work, I used to go into the men's kitchen and ask the man washing up if, when he finished with the last dish, I could bathe in the remaining water. The sink was a big industrial affair, big enough for me to climb in, and the water, if I ignored the floating detritus, was just warm enough for me to close my eyes and think of better days.

I would bathe and shave as often as I could, and it did a great deal to help me remain sane. Like my boots, for me razor blades were essential to keep my dignity. I was always prepared to exchange food or drink in return for a blade. The Germans had a strange distaste for beards, thinking they brought germs and dirt. The last thing I wanted was to attract attention as a 'hygiene risk'.

The prison uniforms were blue and white striped and, because of my continually washing them in dirty water, mine soon became blue and grey. Socks, nderwear and shoes were not issued by the authorities – we had to find our own, as best we could, through the usual means of barter and theft. I always made a priority of keeping my feet protected. I also had a good civilian shirt and a decent pair of trousers.

Many did not have these luxuries, nor did they care about their appearance, and they became covered in lice and sores and eventually lost the will to live. But keeping some sense of dignity allowed me to stay strong enough for me to be useful.

Whenever I could, I would make my way clandestinely to the Grosse Ghetto of German Jews. In those times they lived in hope, believing the Nazi propaganda that they would be saved while we, their fellow Jews, were headed for oblivion. We knew this lie for what it was – we had seen the SS and their Latvian allies slaughter Jews with no regard to where they came from. As far as Adolf Hitler was concerned we were all destined for the same brutal ending.

There was, of course, still an affinity between Jews from all over Europe and visits between the two camps were sometimes allowed. When the authorities refused us permits, we had our own 'private' entry, through a carefully camouflaged hole in the barbed wire in a dark shadowy corner of Daugavpilsstrasse.

The Grosse Ghetto was, to put it bluntly, where my friends and I went to play sport and to enjoy other pleasures of the flesh with German Jewish women. The first was part of the official curriculum but the second strongly verboten! We would meet the German women when we were marched together as a group through the streets of Riga to our designated work. Relationships grew and developed behind the barbed wire and trysts were made. Romance, yes, but romantic it was not.

The women who had relationships with us Latvians

were looked down upon by the elders in their Ghetto, but I suspect they were quick enough to ask for their share of the food and other presents we took on our visits for the girls' favours.

With my physical work for the Germans and a little exercise when circumstances allowed, I kept myself fit, with circuit training, shadow boxing and sparring when a partner could be found. It was clearly an unusual sight for Germans and Jews alike.

The two chiefs of police who controlled the camps met regularly and at one of these meetings, the idea of a fight between Ghetto inmates was suggested by my friend and saviour, Rudy Harr. Rudy was more than an ex-boxer – he had worked as a professional coach and fight promoter, and had a good promoter's sense of how to turn a match into a spectacle. He knew I had some experience in the ring and he proposed a match between me and the German Werner Samuel, a one-time professional middleweight champion. The idea was quickly accepted by the German Jews, who saw this as a very one-sided fight, a professional against a young amateur with extremely limited experience. It would be good for their morale, they believed, to see their champion win what they expected to be an easy victory.

Before the Ghetto, the prospect of such a match would have terrified me, but now it gave me something to cling to, something to live for. Suddenly I did not feel I was helpless. I could actually fight a

German without fear of execution, regardless of the outcome!

My friends rallied round, borrowing, begging and stealing all the food they could to support me as I trained. For a brief time, our lives as slaves to the invading army and grim workdays in the Ghetto were almost forgotten as I prepared for the bout. There was no ring to practise in and sparring partners were limited to say the least, life was tough enough as it was without being hit about the head and body for fun – there were plenty of Germans and Latvians who would do that, secure in the knowledge that they wouldn't get hit back – but I was able to work on my strength and fitness, skipping, hammering a home-made punch bag, lifting rubble and pushing heavy handcarts. It no longer felt like manual work but serious training. I looked upon the upcoming exhibition match as a title fight.

The contest was arranged in the German camp, of course, and I was not allowed to have too many supporters amongst those watching the first fight. No one liked us Latvian Jews, not the Latvians, the Germans or the German Jews, who, while not thought of as part of the so-called Master Race, were definitely seen as a considerable cut above us.

The fight was organised as well as possible and, from somewhere, they found us gloves and head protectors to offer a semblance of normality to the event. There was no great emphasis on formal rules, but if I remember rightly the fight was set at three rounds for my benefit, with the referee to make the decision on points if there was no knockout.

I found an old pair of khaki shorts, some weather-worn but heavy socks and stuffed them down the front of my pants as a makeshift groin protector. No points were to be awarded for style or fashion, after all. A piece of rubber cut roughly to size made for an adequate gum shield – I had more important things on my mind than protecting my teeth. The ring was dragged outdoors from our old gymnasium, where I used to train, and into the middle of the courtyard. It crossed my mind that such was the state of the equipment it would be a harsh landing if I were knocked over, despite the canvas covering.

That ring was a lonely place as I prepared myself in my corner. I looked into the sea of faces at the German soldiers, the Kapos, the German Jews ... they didn't like me and I didn't like them.

Then there was my little clutch of supporters!

In my corner was my faithful young friend Osherke (Osha to me and his friends), the boy I had rescued off the streets of Riga when he was being marched to his death, Zotke, the suave David Ravdin, Kalika, Sroya Scholomson and others from the periphery of our close-knit group, the Strong Ones. It was haughtily assumed by the Germans there was no way I was going to beat their famous champion and the home crowd were soon on their feet cheering, stamping and shouting as he emerged from his corner like a hurricane, pummelling me with head and body shots. He was quick and clever and as an amateur who had never fought more than three rounds against boxers of my own class before, I was taken by surprise.

Two left jabs stopped me in my tracks and a right hook put me down on one knee. I could feel the blood gathering in my nasal passages and the roar of the crowd echoed painfully in my ears. Osha and my friends were urging me to get up and fight on, for this, as far as our little group of Latvian Jews was concerned, was for more than a title. This was about pride and a rare chance to hold our heads high.

The old, cracked canvas beneath my knee felt rough and hard, the punches had hurt and I knew I was in danger of being outclassed, taking damage that would injure me physically, far more than it could hurt our small group's pride.

His left was a tattoo on my face, followed up by stinging rights. I took the blows, and then put my chin in the way of a right hook and hit the canvas with a sickening thump. The partisan crowd were on their feet, cheering and throwing their hats in the air. It looked like it was going to be over quickly.

I shook my head to clear my fogged brain, thumbed the trickle of blood from my nose and climbed back to my feet on the count of eight. I saw the only way that I could fight back was to go on the attack, take him by surprise and rough him up a bit.

Good thinking, but before I could put my plan into action he put me down again!

He had already dumped me to the floor, once onto the seat of my pants, and once to my knees, much to the joy of the guards and the German Jews. But their cheering gave me fresh determination and I bored in and began to make my advantage in weight tell as I took the fight to him, using my raw strength, rather than the more refined techniques I had learned as an amateur. The crowd did not like this sudden shift in my approach, especially when I used my head, the odd elbow and one or two illegal blows to his kidneys and the back of his neck. The Germans began to boo and jeer, screaming out loud. I was too rough and too dirty for their champion. If they couldn't see me knocked out they wanted to see me kicked out and disqualified.

It was music to my ears and, with the referee uncertain how to react to this sudden turn of events, the adrenalin began to flow. I'd heard that the referee was experienced, but best of all he was impartial. I didn't know the man but am certain that he was a non-Jewish Latvian.

I drew Samuel into the sort of mauling, street-corner fight he neither wanted nor expected and as I threw my hardest punches I could feel his strength draining away. I doubted his diet was as good as mine. Perhaps our foraging and stealing food was better than that of the German Jews, but as I began to push him around the ring I knew this was now my fight to win or lose. I knocked him down for the first time with a classic left uppercut after trapping him in his own corner. I immediately piled on the pressure when he staggered to his feet, putting him down a second time with a right cross that connected with the point of his jaw. This time he stayed down. The Latvian referee seemed, to my imagination, to extend the count for as long as he could but it was still not long enough.

The atmosphere around the ring had turned silent and threatening as he struggled to regain his feet, then bitter and furious as the count ground its way to ten. Only my little band of friends and followers were pleased with the result. The German crowd were not at all happy seeing their champion felled by a novice. But novice was not what they called me. The vitriol and bile came spilling out – but I didn't care. I had struck a blow, if only a small one, for the oppressed Latvian Jews. I did not even contemplate the consequences.

A coat was thrown over my shoulders and my friends hustled me out of the gates to the jeers of the opposition fans and back to the sanctuary of our own quarters. I never thought I would be so pleased to see our Ghetto.

The organisers of what had been intended as little more than an exhibition of German strength and dominance were appalled by the result, and soon decided something had to be done to restore the delicate balance between the two camps. They dismissed the knockout as a fluke and arranged a rematch.

This time they made sure my opponent trained hard and ate well, giving Werner every possible advantage. Yet I beat him again, as this time I knew for sure I could. Only a boxer could understand the psychological advantage of facing an opponent you've defeated before. Werner had the skill and the experience but I had strength, superior weight, and youthful determination.

As so often happens between adversaries in sport and particularly in the noble art, we were enemies when we first climbed into the ring, but over time Werner and I became firm friends. Strip away the trappings and he was just one of the guys, in as big a fix as I was. This wasn't part of the war; it was sport, and something we had in common.

In desperation the Germans searched for and found another boxer to show the local boy's successes were nothing more than freak chance. This one might have been bigger than Werner Samuel but he was not nearly as talented as my newfound friend and I stopped him in the third round of our only fight. He was big but he was slow and scarcely landed a glove on me as I kept him at arms' length and then hammered him to the body when we closed in. I didn't even bother to discover his name before the fight and, unlike Werner, our paths never crossed again.

I was hated for beating their boxers but I did what I

had to do. If I had not fought my hardest they would have shown me no mercy. After defeating Werner twice and then stopping their next contender, those in charge of the German Jews' Ghetto and the Latvian Ghetto put an end to boxing amongst inmates. Even training and sparring were banned as the Germans lost interest in boxing and turned to football as a sporting recreation, so resentful were they of their plan's failure to prove German superiority, even amongst Jews.

But I had made a good, new friend in Werner Samuel and grown closer to the man who made the match, Rudy Harr. As one of the senior guards in the German Ghetto he was a useful friend to have, although there was no ulterior motive on my part. I just liked and respected the man. He was brave and loyal, saving my life on more than one occasion. Boxing had not only kept me going – it had helped keep me alive. I was lucky, I was young, fit and not bad looking as well as being a boxer and I had several girlfriends. Winning the three fights might not have suited the men in their camp but it did me no harm at all with the German girls. I took advantage of my new celebrity. It was human nature and I was able to visit them in their apartments. Some of the German Jews were not happy about it at all.

By a strange coincidence I was not the only boxer in our Ghetto, there was also Schlomo Zlotnikow, a gentle giant of a man and a native of Riga. He was a natural sportsman and, apart from boxing, he was another like me, who enjoyed swimming in the river and the sea, even in wintertime. He was also a keen horseman and, surprisingly, an ice skater.

I would have no doubt sparred with him and maybe even boxed exhibitions but the tragic death of an opponent in the ring had ended his promising career. Instead he worked off his excess energy in a leather tannery, hauling huge piles of hides with little or no apparent effort. Like me, his strength was the source of his survival under German rule. He had no love for the Russians either for his father had been inducted into the Russian army when he was just a child. He and his wife lost touch and she and Schlomo spent seven years scouring St Petersburg and the surrounding countryside trying to get word of him, but in vain.

They returned to Riga and when he was thirteen Schlomo had left school to support his mother. There were other similarities between us when he was taken into the Riga Ghetto, where he lost his wife and twin sons when he was taken to a labour camp.

The coincidences did not end there for he was, like me, an inveterate thief who stole potatoes for himself and his friends. When caught he was brutally tortured as the SS tried to get him to give up those he had been stealing with. He was both stubborn and strong and although his legs were blackened from ankle to knee and his ear lobes burned back to his skull he would not give up his friends.

He refused to believe that his family was dead and was certain that he would eventually rejoin them despite the evidence against their survival. He survived and was sent to a displaced persons camp in Germany where he met Esther Lichtenbaum, who had just spent more than three years in Bergen-Belsen, the same camp that my future wife Hela passed through and many didn't survive. He even went back to Riga where he discovered his house had been used by Nazi High Command and finally confirmed his wife and twins had been killed.

His new wife Esther was from Warsaw and she smuggled him into Poland, where foreign Jews were not welcome, but they quickly moved on to Gdynia and then to Israel in 1951 as they struggled with the anti-Semitism still common in Poland.

Then it was on to America where he was a busboy at Ratner's Restaurant, in New York; he cleaned houses in Los Angeles and somehow he managed to bury the past and began a new life in America – where I bumped into him in Los Angeles!

He never spoke of his dead twins, not even to mention their names to his daughter Annette Segal who became great friends with my son Mike. The first time he mentioned them was when Annette gave birth to a boy and he broke down in tears because, he said, the baby looked so much like the twins. Although he was a little older than me, he was born in 1907, we boxed at the same club and knew each other well in Riga and it was remarkable when we discovered each other alive and well in the USA.

CHAPTER SIX

THE EMPTY GRAVE

Every day, I knew, could be my very last on God's earth. There was always unrelenting, gut-wrenching tension. What was, in the dreadful circumstances we found ourselves in, an ordinary day, could turn into your last on the whim of someone you had never met, never looked in the eye, someone from another country who had no right to even be in your life, let alone decide when it should end.

The Germans had a quota. So many of us Jews had to be killed day-by-day, week-by-week and month-by-month until we were all gone, the *Final Solution*, to satisfy Adolf Hitler. At any given moment you could become part of some faceless Nazi's quota of Jews to be exterminated that day, just to keep their records straight.

Inevitably it happened to me, right out of the blue. It was as normal a day as you could get in those strange

and violent times. I was working for the Germans
with a group of other Latvian Jews in the railway
yards just beyond the Maskavas District where we
lived, soaked to the skin through my threadbare blue
and grey striped uniform by the steady drizzle from
the leaden skies above Riga.

It was hard work and uncomfortable but at least
I had the pleasure of dry feet. One thing my father
had always taught me was the value of good shoes or
boots. I never forgot. I would happily swap precious
food or other stolen goods in return for a strong pair
of boots that were a good fit. A bottle of vodka for
a pair of strong German leather boots was a good
deal as far as I was concerned and there was always a
greedy Latvian who, once he knew what you wanted,
would come up with the right size for vodka, a gold
coin or a piece of jewellery. Nothing is more uncomfortable than splashing about in puddles in railway
yards, replacing the big wooden sleepers to accom-
modate the German troop and food trains, with shoes
repaired by pieces of cardboard that soaked through
and left the feet cold and wet.

I was silently congratulating myself on my warm,
dry feet as we lifted yet another sleeper into place
when a German truck splashed up to us and a grumpy
German soldier, well wrapped up in his greatcoat,
ordered my group to climb on board with no word
about where we were going or what we were supposed
to do.

Fear grasped my guts and squeezed hard. This was not normal. This wasn't something that happened when we were on a shift like this. I feared the worst and so did those who were picked out with me at random. The journey was bumpy and short but it became patently obvious what lay in store for us when the truck pulled into the Jewish Cemetery on Liksnas Street at the corner of the Big Ghetto, in the triangle formed by Kölner, Bielefelder and Lauvas streets. We knew all about this last resting ground. It was the cemetery built in 1725 on the outskirts of the city, south east of Riga. Before that Jews were forced to take their dead 40 kilometres to Jelgava, the closest Jewish resting ground, or as far away as Poland.

This was a one-way journey. Our work was finished, not only for the day – but forever, it seemed. There were only two reasons to be taken to the cemetery, one was to bury dead Jews, and the other was to be executed by the Kommandant or one of his underlings on his orders. This was not a punishment execution, the soldiers did not even have a list of those to be killed. This was simply keeping up with the demands from Berlin, ensuring the quota was met.

I looked around, sure that this would be my last day on earth. What goes through your mind at such a time? Maybe, I thought, it would mean meeting up with my mother Chaya and lost brother Fima, perhaps this would bring peace at last. But I was far from ready for such despair and I felt my muscles spasm as I prepared myself for what would be my last stand. The bell was about to ring for the final round. What did I have left?

What could I do? Succumb with eyes closed, as so many did in their despair, or go out with a knockout punch? I looked around the graveyards of the dead and silently promised them I would not go down with a whimper as I saw the white faces and shivering bodies of those around me and the indifferent attitude of the Germans with their rifles and their cruel eyes.

It was a cold, grey miserable afternoon, with the light failing fast as winter closed in. I shivered when, in the near distance, I could see the local fire department, our own Latvian people, hosing down dead bodies in the open mortuary. The dead Jews were being washed with disinfectant to avoid an epidemic. The Germans were insistent on such measures. They were sticklers for cleanliness and very wary of spreading disease through the many dead bodies they had scattered across our countryside. They knew what they were doing, having done it so often and, of course, it was for their own protection. The last thing they wanted was to catch some life-threatening disease from us, alive or dead.

The Latvian Guards were not far from where we stood, but cared nothing. It was something they had seen many times before and, anyway, they were regularly even worse than the Germans and fiercely anti-Semitic. We had fought with them often enough long before the Germans arrived. Their hatred had increased in 1905 when the Jews were blamed for provoking riots by the enemies of the revolution against Tsar Nicholas II and again in 1917 during the Bolshevik Revolution. They could have even been Kapos. Whoever they were they ignored us completely as we were ushered through the inevitable brown mud to the burial grounds where shovels were thrown to us and we were told to start digging.

We did not need to ask what or where to dig. Everyone understood the order was to excavate a deep pit that would then serve as our mass grave when they lined us up and fired … if we were lucky. If we sustained a non-fatal wound we would still be thrown in along with our dead fellow prisoners. I almost smiled when the thought popped into my head that the Germans would have to fill in the grave themselves if we were all in the pit, dead. Although, on reflection, I guess they would simply have whistled over a group of Kapos to do their dirty work.

I considered my options. At least I had a weapon in my hands with the sharp edged spade and maybe I could take at least one of these bastards with me before I went.

I glanced sideways to see if any of my countrymen were feeling the same way. Judging by their bowed heads and sad faces they were resigned to their fate but any hopes of group action disappeared in a moment when another camouflaged military truck splashed its way towards us and disgorged a unit of SS killers.

We were completely outflanked. Escape was more than impossible and even the hope of striking a single blow for the free world had vanished. One move and we were dead. They would have loved for us to show some resistance. These were the bad bunch, dressed all in black and known as the 'Black Hats', or put more simply – The Death Squad.

These were the professionals. They had already killed so many they would not turn a hair at adding this young Latvian Jew to their list the moment he lifted his shovel above waist height.

But I was damned if I was going to dig my own grave and I was still quietly debating how I should strike when a towering SS man, separate from the newly arrived group, strode purposefully towards us. He stopped and looked directly at me from under the peak of his sleek hat, which covered the upper half of his face, and then turned to talk to the Wehrmacht Unterscharführer (army corporal) who was in charge of our sorry bunch.

The newcomer cut a sinister figure, at least six feet four inches tall, dressed in black from head to the brightly shined toes of his boots and boasting the death's head badge on the sleeve of his tunic, an SS-Hauptsturmführer, which singled him out as one of the captains in the elite death squad.

He pointed to me and told the officer he wanted this

particular Jew for himself. He told the man in charge of the detail he had been looking for me for years and he wanted the pleasure of killing me himself. In way of explanation he spat out that I hated all Germans and we had fought over the issue before the war and now he wanted to kill me himself.

I understood every word but even had I not spoken German, his gestures and expression would have made it obvious what he wanted: me.

The officer shrugged and told him if he didn't kill me then they would and, in any case, they had plenty more to deal with. He turned his attention away from me before scuttling to the shelter of a canvas hut.

The giant, as if reading my mind, knocked the shovel out of my hands as I tightened my grip on the handle. There was no time for last thoughts or memories, only fear, as his vice-like grip tightened on my arm and I was dragged off, stumbling through the puddles, watched by my fearful comrades until I was prodded round a corner into a quiet area of the cemetery away from the rest of the group by the business end of his rifle.

Who was this demon? Why did he want to kill me so badly? What cock-and-bull story was this he had told the officer? I was bemused and baffled. At least it was only one man I faced, and I was preparing to fight this colossus when he lowered his rifle, took off his hat and said quietly: 'Remember me, Nathan?'

I was stunned as I stared into this familiar face. It

was my childhood friend Danny, a constant childhood companion who had followed my boxing avidly.
The years fell away as I recalled how we played sport
together and he always swore he would be willing to
lay down his life for me and any of his Jewish friends,
even though he was a German by blood. He was as
good as his word and as a strong young man he was
always there when someone tried to beat up one of us
or tried to take sexual liberties with a Jewish woman.

Danny was one tough character. When someone
once attacked his girlfriend he took the aggressor
on in a knife fight and lost one of his little fingers.
But the other man lost far more, his life. Not too
many were prepared to challenge his authority after
that episode.

We ate together, drank and womanised together.
We were very, very close.

On one occasion he sided with us in a skirmish
between the Jewish youngsters and a group of his
own *volksdeutsche* at a resort on our summer vacations
on the Gulf of Riga. We sent them back to the city
covered in blood and bandages.

Danny and I had a beautiful life together. There
was always a group of fifteen to twenty of us drinking,
laughing, joking, the sort of thing healthy young men
do together the world over. We were all like brothers,
but especially Danny and I. I knew Danny's mother
and father, in fact all of his family. But I never saw any
of them again. I had no one to tell of his courage and

of his great friendship. He would have been shot had they discovered what he had done.

When war broke out Hitler called all the *volks-deutche* back to Germany and that meant Danny and his family had to leave. Despite the times and the problems we even held a farewell party for him with drinking and dancing until the early hours and that was the last time I saw him until we came face to face in the cemetery.

It was just as though God had sent down an angel.

Danny was very emotional as he grasped me by my shoulders, tears streaming down this strong man's face. He said: 'After I have kissed you goodbye I am going to fire my pistol in the air so that the officer in charge of the detail thinks I have killed you. I am going to give you both of my hands, put your foot in them and I will throw you over the cemetery wall. Then get the hell out of it. They were about to shoot you and put you in the grave you were digging.'

I looked him in the face as the tears, so hard to shed in recent troubled times, mingled with the rain and blinded me. I knew what an incredible chance he was taking when he could have simply walked away and said a prayer for his lost friend. Had an inquisitive German soldier looked around the corner and discovered what was happening Danny would have shot him rather than me. He acted like an older brother and in that moment I found true friendship in the worst of circumstances.

There was an eerie silence about the graveyard. The firemen had finished and the digging in the soft earth was making no discernable noise, at least not in our quiet corner of the cemetery. The wall was made of old rough stone and it was high, very high but with my life at stake I guess I could have jumped it without any assistance.

Danny, who stood two heads taller than me, cupped his hands together, told me to put my dirty boot in them and with a huge heave of his broad shoulders he sent me flying to the top of the wall where I scrambled to regain my balance and then dropped the six or seven feet down to the other side into the soft earth on the edge of Lauvasstrasse.

As I landed I heard Danny fire off his two shots. Everyone in that cemetery must have heard them on that still, damp late afternoon. But I wasn't hanging around to find out and, pulling my soaked clothes around me, I set off, heading back towards the Ghetto. Where else was I to go? I doubted whether the guards would remember me as they rarely looked us in the eye and even when the detail came for the next 'shift' of work the chances were that no one would notice yet another dirty Jew.

No, there was nowhere else for me to go but 'home' to the Ghetto and I raced back as though all the demons of hell were on my back. I hugged the side of Hebräische Begrabnisstrasse (Jewish Cemetery Road); diving into the shrubs every time I heard any movement, before heading cross-country. There were few motorised vehicles but I could guarantee every one of them would be manned by German soldiers, the SS, or Kapos.

At one stage a platoon of soldiers marched past heading goodness knows where. I held my breath as they went within yards of where I crouched in the hedgerow. But there was little chance of them seeing or hearing me in the persistent drizzle. All they wanted to do was get to wherever they were going and into some shelter.

I let out a long sigh of relief after they had gone, waiting until they had totally disappeared from my vision before moving on. When I finally stumbled into the Ghetto I was shaking like a leaf. I knew how close I had come to death and I went straight to our secret basement where there was some vodka hidden and I drank and drank, ripping off my soaked and soiled clothes, until I passed out. I slept the rest of the night like the dead man I should have been.

I never saw or heard from Danny again but I often think of him and wondered what had become of the man who undoubtedly saved my life. Did he survive the war or even that fateful day? If they had demanded to see my body the game would have been up and he would have died in my place. But such was his size and his presence I somehow doubted anyone would have questioned him.

From what I learned later he saved others in the

same sort of way he had rescued me. He had continually put his life on the line, taking incredible risks. I wish I knew if he had survived the war. Somehow I doubt it. He took the risks willingly and happily. He was an intelligent, quick-witted man, a fearless warrior who could, as my reprieve showed, construct life-saving plans on the spot. There is nothing I would like better than to shake his hand once more and thank him, not just for saving my life but for being the best and truest friend a man could have, in a place where there was little warmth or friendship.

CHAPTER SEVEN

CHANGING WEIGHT

I had the will and the wish to keep myself in shape, even if that meant stealing food where and when I could but still, I lost weight. When I was incarcerated in the Ghetto for the first time I weighed a solid, muscular 180 pounds with barely a spare inch of fat on my body.

When I was finally liberated from the concentration camp in Germany, I still had no fat but now I weighed in at barely 105 pounds – and I was amongst the lucky ones. We have all seen those pictures of the liberation of concentration camps where the inmates were little more than a bag of bones.

In boxing terms I had gone from one end of the scale to the other, slimming down from cruiserweight, just below heavyweight, to light flyweight, just a pound above the lowest category of strawweight. The fact I was still fighting fit was a testament to my ability as a thief as much as my athletic prowess.

Training was, by now, impossible as we were little more than slaves. The Germans would delight in parading the Jews to watch them hang one of our countrymen simply for taking a piece of bread or stealing some butter. They didn't need an excuse to commit murder and I was constantly tempting fate with my way of life. But there is no doubt that the discipline of being a boxer, keeping fit and the years of training were the source of my survival. Without them I would not have come through the nightmare.

Boxing was my main interest because I loved the sport so much but I was also doing physical work all the time, lifting excessive weights and picking up heavy, heavy boxes in the warehouses where I worked. All of this helped me to reach a level of fitness that I managed to maintain well into my seventies before a couple of strokes restricted me.

But once you have learned an art or a trade, you don't forget it. I was able to defend myself whenever I was cornered, which was quite often, and I was not willing to be hit without hitting back; no one was going to steal my food from me after I had risked my life stealing it in the first place. Sadly, I had a lot of fights with fellow prisoners. Hungry people are like animals – and so was I. But the difference was I knew how to defend myself and they didn't. Most of the fights were with the German Jews who, even though they were incarcerated and humiliated as we were, still thought themselves superior to us Jews from Eastern

Europe. They were born Germans and thought like Germans, even though their country treated them like pariahs.

The main focus of the day was always food and where we could get more. It has to be said that there was the occasional German who wasn't so bad, more interested in making the war as comfortable as possible for himself until he could return home than causing harm to Ghetto inmates. This applied to the soldiers as well as the German Jews.

There was one in particular, a blue-nosed Sergeant who was a complete drunk. He would regularly ask me if I could 'buy' him a bottle of vodka. He would tell me to take off my Star of David topcoat that I was forced to wear to show my affiliations in public in the Ghetto and go into the town in ordinary slacks and a shirt to find him what he needed. I would gather together a bag and fill it with shoes and clothes liberated from countrymen who had been killed, walk into town and trade with the Latvians to earn enough for a couple of bottles of vodka for the guard and, naturally, some food for myself and my comrades.

The sergeant gave me nothing in return but he turned a blind eye to my stealing food by way of a reward. Anything was better than the slop we were handed in the Ghetto.

One of my regular stopovers on these trips was the house of a lady where I was always given soup … and often a little more. I had my suspicions as to how this charming and attractive woman kept herself healthy and stylish. These were confirmed one day early in our relationship when an SS soldier opened the door and came in as I sat waiting for her in her lounge.

I knew I was in trouble as he cast his eyes across my face. He asked if I was Jewish and I said no, that I was a Latvian. He could not be certain one way or the other unless he made me strip and searched me for a foreskin – quite the reverse of what he had come here for. He suspiciously closed the door and told me to sit in a vacant chair on the other side of the room to him. He turned to me and said: 'Sit there – but remember I am first.'

My lady friend was clearly selling her favours to the Germans and, sure enough, she appeared a while later after seeing off an earlier customer. She took in the situation straightaway and told me to wait till she had finished with the officer.

While she was seeing the other client out of the door the SS man looked me up and down and said ominously: 'I still think you are a Jude.'

I looked him squarely in the eye and told him: 'I don't know what you are talking about.' I was acting, but failing to pull off a convincing performance would have made those words my last lines in this life. But clearly the SS man still had doubts.

He ostentatiously took out his gun and said: 'If I find out you are a Jew I will shoot you here and now.'

My instinct was to run, to get out of there as fast as I could, but flight was not an option. Even had I managed to escape the house and the SS officer's bullets, he had studied my features closely, and would have been able to provide a detailed description to a search party. My benefactor, too, would have been in great danger, and suffered the consequences for entertaining a Jew.

As we stood there, face to face, the lady herself reappeared and spoke quite harshly to the SS man, saying: 'Carl, Carl, get the hell out of here if you ever want to come again. Come back tomorrow when you have calmed down. That is the best way. Remember this guy was here before you and I need his custom, too.'

She was obviously skilled at her profession, for he reluctantly did as he was told and left while she went back into the kitchen and brought me soup that I hungrily mopped up with bread, proper bread, not the stale and rancid crusts that we ate in the Ghetto. She also handed me some bacon that I carefully wrapped up, along with a bottle of vodka for the guard.

We Jews, of course, were not supposed to eat pork, but religious dietary restrictions seemed unimportant in the Ghetto, and Latvian Jews had often, in happier times, indulged in native pork dishes anyway. Me? I would have eaten the entire pig if she had given it to me, snout and all.

I did not enjoy the good lady's other favours that day as we were both too shaken: but the near-miss with the SS officer did not put an end to our relationship. Whenever my tame guard with the blue nose demanded vodka I would make my way to her house, being careful to avoid any other customers.

It may all sound harmless enough now, but at the time, I was treading a narrow line between life and death. My soul was in my feet as I sneaked out of her house, wondering if I would turn a corner and see the SS officer frustrated and enraged that I had foiled his designs, waiting for me.

This constant fear, continually looking over the shoulder for the bullet or the rope, became an everyday part of my life or, rather, my survival, with even the most harmless situations quickly developing into life or death epics. One day the SS held a ball in the barracks, eating, drinking and dancing, enjoying everything that was supposed to be denied to us. Our only part in the festivities was that we were detailed to clean up the barracks after the party was over.

I made sure my name topped the list of volunteers. Inevitably, they would leave scraps of meat and unfinished plates, and this, to me, was another chance to fill my belly. It was not a chance I was going to miss but the SS man left in charge spotted me sorting through the scraps and said: 'Listen, I saw what you did. You put to one side some meat that wasn't eaten. I have a big dog outside and I want to have the meat for him.'

I shrugged and said I would take the meat out for his fierce German shepherd dog. He gave me a tray to put the meat on and then told me to take it to his dog, waiting outside the barrack's door. He then said to my disappearing back: 'If I see you eating one single piece of this meat on the way I am going to stand here with my gun and I am going to shoot you like the pig you are and then my dog will eat you.'

I looked down at the meat. I was just as hungry as his dog and although he was threatening me, he had been polite to start with. Perhaps, I thought to myself, he was just testing me, acting the part of the sadist and killer for his own amusement or to impress his SS comrades. I figured he wasn't going to kill me because he would, at the best, be left to clear up the mess and explain himself. I picked up one piece of meat and, in full view of the officer, popped it in my mouth and started chewing.

I tensed, waiting for the bullet – but nothing happened. I had read the situation correctly. He did not say a word as I took what was left of the meat out to his pet. The dog was grateful and rather than biting the hand that fed him, he licked me and got on with his supper, even sharing some of it with me.

Was I brave or just plain stupid? I don't know. But what had I got to lose? My father was, as far as I knew, in Palestine or dead, I didn't know whether my brother Boris was alive or dead fighting the Germans with the Russian army and both my mother and younger brother were already gone.

I had thought to myself, what the hell, if I cannot eat a piece of meat, let him shoot me. Two and two is four. At least it was this time and I didn't bother to ask him why he hadn't pulled the trigger. I just got on with cleaning up the barracks.

CHAPTER EIGHT

THE FREEDOM FIGHTERS

Not everyone was as lucky as me. It did seem at times as though someone up there was looking down on me, keeping me alive time after time when others died for far lesser violations of the rules than my constant stealing. There was yet another remarkable escape when others perished while I survived to fight another day.

I was not on my own in my attitude towards our tormentors and my determination to survive and see them punished for their wicked ways. There were many others like me who were not satisfied just to sit on their backsides, slowly starving or waiting to be taken away and executed to maintain the Nazi's bloody quota.

Within the Ghetto, some of us who thirsted for revenge formed a small resistance group. Whenever we could find a little spare time, we used what was left of our precious strength and failing health to dig out a secret basement under the buildings. It was an ambitious and difficult project even for a professional team but what we lacked in expertise we made up for in enthusiasm. This was our one means of fighting back, and live or die we had resolved to go down fighting.

Deep in the Ghetto we developed a partisan defence group of freedom fighters. When we went to work in the horse and trap to pick up the food for the Ghetto we took the opportunity to trade and bring in guns and other weapons. The Latvians would sell their mothers for money, so they were easy enough to buy providing we had something to offer.

The Latvian Guards were only too aware that they had a group of freedom fighters amongst those remaining in the Ghetto but as long as they could earn from their compatriots' efforts they were unconcerned – unless the Germans should offer them more!

Our aim was to build a tunnel to the woods of Rumbula where so many of the Jewish population of Riga had perished at the hands of the invaders, fuelling our anger, giving added impetus to the urge to fight. There we planned to link up with Russian partisans who operated within the many forests in our area, working to harass and kill as many of the German army as they could. These were not our natural allies and they were often in conflict with other groups of Soviet partisans. Indeed, in the past it had been us they were fighting. But in Riga our aims were the same, getting the Germans out of Latvia by any means possible. It was amongst the trees that our two groups met and discussed ambitious plans to put a spanner in the German war machinery.

Fortunately, we had people who knew what they were doing and we dug out the earth from beneath a huge oven, of all things. The Germans were indiscriminate in who they corralled and we had in our midst engineers, architects, builders and other intelligent men who needed to exercise their minds as much as I needed to exercise my muscles. We erected posts to hold up the tunnel and carefully worked out a system of getting rid of the rubble without drawing attention to ourselves. We put the sand in the huge rubbish bins which the garbage men would empty, throwing their contents on the dump outside the city. If they realised what was going on they said and did nothing to alert the Germans.

We also made sure that the tunnel diggers were well supplied and there was enough water down in the cellar and the tunnel to last us for months. There was also food, with dried bread that would keep for a long time, along with real delicacies of ham, bacon, everything we had been able to steal from our unwelcome and unwanted guests.

One day one of the Russian partisans bravely smuggled himself in, clinging on to the underside of one of the trucks that brought in the supplies for the Germans. A smart move, as the guards were on the lookout for people trying to escape, not would-be infiltrators. We quickly and quietly spirited him into our lodgings, knowing the inevitable outcome if the SS found us. No one would survive such a discovery: not us, not the Russian, and not those who knew – or were suspected of knowing – of our group.

We showed the Russian our secret base and proudly pointed out our tunnel, created with our own hands. It was just wide enough for the biggest of us to crawl through and the hidden exit was exactly opposite the SS Command post.

It was stunning to think we had done so much, without anyone discovering our excavations. I suspect we got away with it, again, because they did not expect us to fight back. To the SS, the idea of a Jewish resistance group in the Ghetto would probably have seemed funny.

The Russian, one of the guerrilla group's leaders, saw no use for the tunnel, but was interested in us as reinforcements for his dwindling band of freedom fighters who had suffered casualties in their running battles. If the Germans could ever pinpoint their positions they would parachute in Stormtroopers to wipe them out.

He told us he would talk to each of us individually and decide who he would take back to the woods to help the partisans in their struggle. When he came to me he took one look and immediately told me that he couldn't take me with him. Distraught, I asked him why and he told me to look in the mirror, because I looked 'too much like a Jew'! I was not blond enough for him and far too easy to pick out, even in a crowd.

Only two of us were rejected, left behind while the others departed with the Russian, hidden in a supply truck along with the weapons, machine guns amongst them, we had managed to acquire. The two of us who remained watched them drive away in absolute despair. We longed to be with them, to finally have a chance to fight back properly, with arms and experienced soldiers as comrades against the Germans who had butchered our families and enslaved us. I have rarely felt as lonely as I did in that moment.

Once more, however, luck was with me. Unfortunately for our colleagues the Germans had been tipped off that something was being smuggled out in the trucks. Although they let them pass through the gates, they followed, and when the truckload of hidden partisans and weaponry reached the edge of town they stopped them and demanded to see their papers.

In isolation the papers would probably have passed muster, particularly if others had the genuine item but these were, of course, all forgeries and the entire group was machine-gunned to death while still trapped in the trucks.

Our boys tried valiantly to defend themselves but all fourteen of them were slaughtered, along with the Russian partisan, where they stood or sat.

It did not end there. The Germans brought the bloodied corpses, riddled with bullets, back where they came from and threw them into the square in the centre of the Latvian Ghetto along with everything that they had taken with them, apart from the guns, as an example of what would happen to the rest of us if we tried to escape.

They then rounded up the Latvian Jewish police, whom they assumed had to know about the escape plan, and murdered them where they stood. Forty Latvian policemen died at that moment. Murdered in cold blood in Tin Square on 31 October 1942. Another massacre.

But, incredibly, still I somehow survived – this time for looking too Jewish!

It was a sad, sad day and we thought then that there was truly no way to escape alive. We never used that apartment or the tunnels beneath them ever again. They were our memorials to all the innocents who had died that black day.

This was no death camp, not even a labour camp in the true sense of the word, but so many people died there, murdered by the Germans and their Latvian Nazis. Their cruelty knew no bounds and after our escape attempt they introduced a ritual and every single day afterwards they would hang one of our people at Tin Square by the gates of the Ghetto where we had to pass on our way to work, as a chilling reminder of who held the upper hand.

CHAPTER NINE

THE LIFE AND DEATH
OF HERR HARR

Ours was a small world within our capital city. The rest of the globe was on fire but, apart from the news bulletin from a hidden wireless, it was hard to keep in touch with events in the World War beyond our double barbed wire. All we could see was that Latvia and our fate were very much in German hands. The Allied war effort seemed faraway, irrelevant to our predicament.

In fact, though, the Allied troops were not as distant as we thought. It was not the combined Russian and Latvian resistance that eventually forced a change of thinking in Riga but the creeping front of the real war. The Allies were winning and beginning to turn the tide. As the fighting drew closer, so the Germans, along with their prisoners, were forced into retreat.

This meant we were removed from the hated Ghetto and into concentration camps deeper in Latvia. There were 'Death Marches' all over Europe as prisoners were moved or murdered by the Germans.

Ironically, the Nazis closed the Ghetto at the very moment when we had once more stolen, bought and bartered enough guns for us to start thinking of rising up against our despised tormentors. We thought they would be so preoccupied with saving their own hides from the advancing Russians and the Allies that they would not be too concerned with a small group of armed desperadoes, and might even let us escape.

But the timing was against us. When they came to round us up for transport we were too far away from our weapons to arm ourselves and make our stand, and there they lay in hiding, useless, as we were taken out. It was heartbreaking to think of all that effort gone to waste. All those guns, the ammunition, the food, the vodka and the bits and pieces we had hoarded for exchange with the Latvian magpies. This was starting to be a familiar pattern.

Now, instead of hopes of escape, it was out of the frying pan and into the fire, a fire that made the days back in the Ghetto seem like a vacation by comparison. Now there was no chance of boxing, football or a fling with women from the German Ghetto. We were taking another giant stride towards the abyss.

In the spring of 1943 the Nazis built another concentration camp a short distance from the Riga

Ghetto. This was in Kaiserwald or, in Latvian terms, Mežaparks. It was an expensive and very beautiful part of Latvia with posh villas for the wealthy.

We were moved in the summer, June, and needless to say we passed straight through Mežaparks and arrived to the sight of a camp surrounded by electrified fences, two rows of barbed wire and watchtowers manned by armed German soldiers. It was a similar camp to the Ghetto, a little farther inland than Riga, in King's Woods. That's where they purpose built this wooden camp, complete with hospital, morgue, men's and women's barracks alongside the railway track. It was a concentration camp except there were woods around. It certainly wasn't as bad as some of the concentration camps in Poland and Germany and was not officially a death camp, although plenty were killed in its short, shameful life.

The inevitable Kapos greeted us off the trucks, screaming at us to strip and shoved us into the showers. This time I was not worried, if they had wanted to gas us they would have done so back in Riga and saved the petrol!

We were then given our clothes, wooden clogs, blue and grey striped uniform and a cap. There were no pants or socks and I knew I would have to procure those myself, as usual.

We were each given a prison number but it was not tattooed on our arms or legs and was quickly forgotten as far as I was concerned. The Germans obviously had a thing about numbers. This reception took place in the women's barracks but we were soon chased from there by the Kapos and into our own building.

There were probably fifty people in a small area, a long wooden hut with locked doors and a sentry always on duty. The Germans were sticklers for cleanliness and had facilities for washing and cleaning themselves. But they weren't so bothered about us and there were just a couple of showers between all of us.

Unfortunately when we moved, Cukurs's rival for the title of 'Butcher of Riga', Eduard Roschmann, arrived to take charge of affairs. He made sure the discipline was strict, that we were without privacy, clothed in prisoner's uniforms and with shaved heads.

Any thoughts of escape were quickly extinguished for even had we found our way beyond the razor wire and the guards' guns we were quickly identifiable.

We had left the Riga Ghetto at a good time for us and a bad time for those left behind. The camp was gradually being run down with the sick, older people and children transferred to Auschwitz in November 1943, a camp whose name was whispered because of its reputation.

Fortunately the SS had been commissioned by a Germany Company, Lavis Engineering of Halle to build a hanger at the local airport. The Germans selected a group of ten to build it and I quickly volunteered.

It was no easy job as we worked shifts either from

8 a.m. to 6 p.m. or 6 p.m. to 8 a.m., we were beaten regularly and fed just enough to keep us working. The Nazi philosophy was to weaken the spirit so that rebellions would not be organised. But there were opportunities out of the camp to find food meant for our German guards and, as usual, the Strong Ones got by.

We were not the first in the Kaiserwald complex; we were preceded by several hundred German convicts, the Kapos. They lay in wait for us when we arrived and their sport was to beat the hell out of us whenever the opportunity presented itself. After the liquidation of the Riga Ghettos, along with those of Liepaja, Dvinsk and Vilna, most of the few survivors were deported to our new camp and eventually all the remaining Jews living in Latvia were incarcerated in the camp or one of its smaller offshoots.

After that came the Hungarians and Poles from Łódź and by March 1944 there were 11,878 inmates of whom less than a hundred were gentiles. Half the population were female and many of them were kept alive to work for Allgemeine Elektricitäts-Gesellschaft for the production of electrical goods and batteries. Other duties included mining, working farms, factories and maintaining the camp and its satellites.

Our new home was not officially a death camp with gas chambers and burial pits but more a prison populated by slave labourers. This was a camp for strong people, for workers, people with trades – carpenters,

tailors, cooks, whatever – and for those of us considered strong enough it was hard labour in the railway
yards, the airport or any other manual work the
guards demanded.

It may not have been a death camp but death
was still everywhere and the threat constant. This was
graphically displayed to me and my friends with the
cruel death of Rudy Harr, the man who loved boxing
and who had saved my life in the Riga Ghetto.

Being a German looked as though it would
bring continued benefits for my friend Harr as the
Obersturmbannführer Kurt Krause at the German
Ghetto had personally given him a handwritten letter
to the commandant of the Kaiserwald concentration
camp. Harr had earned his position with Krause in a
manner not appreciated by all of the inmates of the
two Ghettos, ingratiating himself with the SS leadership in our Ghetto.

Krause was self-important and travelled around in
a shiny black limousine driven by his adjutant Max
Gymnich, a Gestapo man from Cologne. Gymnich
was an even bigger bastard than Krause, although
not with quite as much power. He was guilty of
many murders and responsible for directing an inhuman approach to the prisoners. Gymnich personally
selected candidates for 'deportation', telling them
that they were heading for the fish tinning factory in
Bolderaa – a factory they never reached.

He outlasted Krause and took over the driving

and other duties with Untersturmführer Eduard Roschmann, the last commandant of the Riga Ghetto. Later he was to feature in the book *The Odessa File* by Frederick Forsyth and was played by Maximilian Schell in the film adaptation of the bestseller. Many complain his portrayal as a monster was exaggerated, and the dedicated Nazi-hunter Simon Wiesenthal, who featured in the book and film, advising Forsyth as he wrote, eventually admitted he had used the fictional *Odessa File* not to record history, but to trap Roschmann, who had survived the war and fled to Argentina. The then-West German government did file for extradition in 1974, but Roschmann died in Paraguay before the various appeals could all be heard. Wiesenthal suspected that he had in fact escaped again, and said 'I wonder who died for him?'

I was gone from the Ghetto by the time Roschmann took over, and know only what I have heard of him from a handful of survivors, none of it good, and all of it explaining why, after the success of *The Odessa File*, he came to be known as 'The Butcher of Riga'. I am only glad I never saw his face.

But I do remember Krause, whose very presence was enough to chill the strongest of hearts. Whenever word spread that Krause and Gymnich were on the prowl with their dog, the Ghetto streets would empty as we hid in our rooms. One of my fellow survivors wrongly identified the hated Krause as Karl Wilhelm Krause who was, apparently, Hitler's personal valet and had no connection with Riga. No one who met Krause would ever forget him or mistake him for anyone else.

One fateful day Rudy Harr was on detail from the Sachsen Transport unit at the Prager Gate with a Latvian SS guard when the commandant's car arrived in Ludzuziela. Krause climbed out in front of the Kommandantur (the Kommandant's office), leaving his driver Gymnich sitting in the car. But when he strutted up to the Prager Gate he found himself ordered to stop by a drunken Latvian guard on duty. Krause, as was his nature, was enraged and lunged at the guard, swearing and threatening to hang him in Tin Square there and then.

The guard, too drunk to be fearful, swung his rifle off his shoulder intent on shooting Krause, but Harr rushed forward and knocked the rifle to one side, deflecting the bullet as he wrestled the man to the ground. The guard again managed to get off another round but, once more, it went wide of its mark before Harr and the now active Gymnich violently restrained and killed him.

There is no doubt that Harr's prompt action and great strength saved the life of Krause and as a reward he was immediately promoted to police chief of the German Ghetto. He was also given his own house on Ludzuziela and became the highest ranked officer in the Ordnungsdienst (Jewish Ghetto Police). He was, from that moment onwards, Krause's man and therefore untouchable by Germans and Latvians alike.

The letter he was given when we were moved on amounted to a reference recounting what a decent man he was, a good and honourable person ... even though he was a Jew!

It looked to be Herr Harr's passport to a comfortable life for the remainder of the war as the letter stressed he should be looked after. But those words, remarkable as they were from the SS, meant nothing when we came to Kaiserwald. When he handed over the letter the Kapos laughed at him and then, in front of all of us, German and Latvian Jews alike, the sadists dragged him into the stinking communal toilets, where everyone was stripped of their dignity as fifty prisoners at a time did their business, threw him into the pit underneath and drowned him in faeces.

This was the man who had saved my life and I had to watch him die, yelling and screaming as he drowned in shit. It was a horrific spectacle, and one that filled me with guilt: the man had saved my life, and yet again, I could do nothing for him.

If life had been hard at the Riga Ghetto it was infinitely harder in the new camp. The prisoners were woken up as dawn broke and lined up like soldiers, counted off into groups of around thirty and despatched by truck or on foot to do whatever job needed to be done that day. It could be anything from the nerve-jangling digging of graves, which always raised the question of whether they would be our own when we were finished, to cultivating the land and growing vegetables. We filled in bomb craters at the airport, unloaded the transport planes and aircraft full of provisions, clothes and whatever else was being brought in for the German troops.

There was no dignity allowed. The Kapos screamed at us as the dawn broke to make sure we were awake and were forced to double march to work. It was made clear we were little more than slaves and they made certain we remained afraid for our lives. I, like everyone else, did what I was told. The alternative was a bullet in the head.

It was a new location but still the same in terms of the deprivation and the limited food. If you didn't steal you went hungry and if caught stealing you were executed. It was as simple as that. It was not the life for a weak or a sick person. I was grateful once again for my youth and that I still had a measure of fitness to draw upon, albeit dwindling rapidly along with my weight.

There were other tasks as they also sent us to work digging the turf for fuel for their fires. There are many forests in the Baltic area around Russia, Latvia, Lithuania and Estonia and over the centuries many trees died and fell to the ground and from this rotting wood the locals, Latvians in particular, dug out lumps for their slow burning fires.

We were forced to dig for this fuel for two months, standing up to our ankles and sometimes our knees in ice cold water, digging and digging without eating or drinking properly. What really hurt was that we were digging to keep the Germans warm while we froze in the effort. It was a demanding job and once again my fitness helped me to survive – I even regained some lost stamina from all the exercise. Others were not so lucky.

Happily neither my courage nor my light fingers had deserted me and both the airport and the railway station presented opportunities for me to steal food, which I always shared with my fellow sufferers once I had fed myself. I was taking huge risks and, almost needless to say, I was soon caught. Yet once again I escaped with my life intact. Someone up there clearly liked me more than I could have dared imagine.

I was stopped, challenged and discovered by a German conscript and he dragged me off to his senior officer to proudly report his capture of a thief. Instead of being executed on the spot, I was thrown into a dank, dark basement with two aggressive dogs. They seemed to be as hungry as I was and not averse to a little kosher meat, as they ripped at me with their fangs. My uniform was soon in shreds, my hands covered with bite marks as I fought to hold them off. Clearly no one would have cared if I died under the assault from the two animals. Maybe that was the plan.

This was inhuman. How could one man treat another like this and for what? For stealing a piece of stale, mildewed bread or a slice of curdled butter that no self-respecting German or his dogs would have touched.

It was not difficult to work out the Germans' plan of campaign. They were there to demoralise us and keep us hungry. They intended to eventually kill all the Jews, but to keep some of us working for their war effort while they still needed the manpower. This was part of that programme and I was right in the middle of it.

Somehow, I survived the dogs and the hunger and, for no apparent reason, I was released to rejoin my fellow prisoners who could not believe my good fortune. The bite marks were a small price to pay for my life.

CHAPTER TEN

SPILVE

One morning I and a group of inmates, a mix of both Latvian and German Jews, were suddenly informed we were leaving the Kaiserwald camp immediately. We were hustled out with only the clothes we stood in and given no time to pack any of our possessions.

The SS guards herded us onto a truck, accompanied by two of their own guards, and we were driven through the inner city of Riga and five kilometres out to a suburb called Spilve, best known for its airport.

There we were taken straight to an abandoned brewery which had been converted into a barrack camp, consisting of a handful of brick buildings encompassed by a high brick wall. We entered through an old wrought iron gate which had been covered over with sheet metal so that no one could see in. It was guarded day and night by the SS, yards away from their Kommandant.

We were quick-marched into our quarters and I was fortunate that my group, the Strong Ones, had managed to stay together. There I was with Zotke, Osha, David Ravdin and Leon Kalika in yet more new quarters.

Again it looked bleak, especially when the reasonable Kommandant, SS officer Schumacher, was replaced by SS-Rapportführer Gustav Sorge, otherwise known as Iron Gustav. He had been shipped from the notorious Sachsenhausen Camp north of Berlin in Brandenburg, where he was known to be one of the cruellest guards in Germany, quite a reputation considering some of the sadistic criminals he was compared to. At his war crimes trial it was claimed that 100,000 were put to death in the camp.

We heard that Sorge was moved to Spilve on the orders of the Reichsführer Heinrich Himmler himself for stealing gold from the Nazi treasure chest – and to think we could be put to death for stealing a piece of stale bread!

His humour had not been improved by his demotion and the ever-present German shepherd dog by his side allied to his furious temper made him a terrifying sight. Often he would release his dog to roam amongst us during roll call. It was a vicious animal and scared even the bravest dog lovers amongst us.

At first, conditions at Spilve had been a little better

than those at Kaiserwald – but not by much. When the SS took over the camp from the Wehrmacht's civilian administration, things rapidly deteriorated. Sorge was assisted by Kroschel and Blatterspiegel with the monster Xaver Apel in overall control. If ever a man deserved the title 'psychopath', then it was Apel. Once sentenced to life imprisonment in Berlin, the Gestapo decided to make use of him, and the stories of his sadism are almost too sick to believe. He raped prisoners at will, and if he found a worker to be too slow, or ill, would throw them bodily into the Daugava River. Once, an inmate who had lost his appetite to dysentery gave his meagre rations to a fellow prisoner: for this 'crime', he was thrown into a huge kettle, boiling water for the camp's 'coffee'. The 'coffee' was served as normal, from this same water in which a sick and starving man had died.

We had bunks in our rooms while the food was still the same watery soup and stale bread. The hygiene, however, was even worse than Kaiserwald's and many prisoners suffered severely from lice. Far from helping clean them up, the Nazis used them in experiments with no obvious purpose, forcing five Jewish prisoners to feed their lice daily with their own blood for twenty minutes so they could be put under the microscope at the Institute of Medical Zoology in nearby Kleist.

The work was also hard, unloading trainloads of rocks and sand and, if we were really unlucky, bombs

Nathan's brothers, Boris and Ephraim.

Nathan's parents, Mordechai and Chaye. Separated before the invasion, Nathan and his father were, remarkably, reunited in Palestine after the war.

A rare photograph of some of the Shapow family.

In July 1941 Riga was invaded. Those who survived the first wave of massacres were imprisoned in Riga's Ghetto, set up in the very suburb Nathan had grown up in.

The Butcher of Riga: Rivalling Herberts Cukurs for the title, Eduard Roschmann was the brutal commandant of the Riga Ghetto.

The famous refugee ship *Exodus*, with some 4,500 survivors of the Nazi camps on board and now under the control of the British, finally docks at Haifa. Prevented from landing, the refugees were forced to return to Germany, provoking a worldwide outcry.

ABOVE Nathan (back row, right) with his 'new' family in Palestine, his father having remarried there. Nathan has his arm on the girl he nearly married.

RIGHT In the midst of all the fighting Nathan found lasting love with fellow concentration camp survivor, Hela.

ABOVE Israel, 1948. Nathan (extreme right, arm outstretched) and fellow soldiers welcome the arrival at Lod Airport of a Czechoslovakian plane, bringing desperately needed rifles and ammunition.

BELOW A pause in the fighting. Nathan and his unit on the road to Jerusalem.

ABOVE Menachem Begin (left), leader of the extreme military group, the Irgun, which Nathan Shapow joined, and Abraham Stern, leader of the even more radical Stern Gang.

BELOW Fawzi el Kaukji, commander of the Arab Liberation army, rallies Arab villagers.

ABOVE After bitter fighting and many losses, Jewish forces finally take the Castel, the strategic hill that overlooked and commanded the road to Jerusalem.

BELOW On 14 May 1948, the State of Israel is proclaimed by David Ben-Gurion, who was to be Israel's first Prime Minister.

LEFT Nathan with his wife Hela, son Mike and daughter Adina.

BELOW Nathan reunited with friends from Riga.

from the closed railway cars. We were always timed by the guards who demanded we worked at double quick time. It was also very cold, much too cold to work in our uniforms. We needed thick jackets and ski caps, but these were not provided so we made do as best we could with whatever we could find, wrapping old carpets around our legs and tying them in place with wire. Not much of a fashion statement but it kept some of the cold out.

Sorge and the SS guards kept well away from us riff-raff and we were watched over by veterans of the Luftwaffe, no longer given flying duties. The worst of the guards was the foreman nicknamed Punzkopf (punch head) who delighted in encouraging us to move faster with the help of an iron bar. We much preferred unloading logs for the sawmill, away from Punzkopf and his seething hatred of Jews.

The contours of the camp were continually changing with the arrival of different groups and our gang was moved onto a second-floor room to make way for a group of Hungarian Jews who had been swept up from the streets of Budapest. There were also prisoners from Lithuania and Czechoslovakia in this cosmopolitan camp, mainly designed to extend the airport for the military. Beatings were frequent, brutal, and often arbitrary, delivered by a bored Kapo or one who wanted to impress a German guard.

Still, we were not in a death camp – unlike the inmates of the nearby Salaspils. Officially a 'Police

Prison and Work Education camp' to the Germans, Salaspils was a death camp, especially for children. Up to 12,000 children went through Salaspils, 7,000 of them Jewish and they were systematically murdered. Many were forced to give blood for German military hospitals.

The Hungarians were originally taken from Budapest to the camp at Auschwitz before a group of them were transferred again, this time by train to Riga, where the women, so they told us, were sexually abused and humiliated by their own Hungarian guards on the way.

The Germans were barred from touching Jewish women and there were very few incidents of sexual harassment or rape although it was not unknown for the senior SS to appoint the prettiest of the Jewish girls as 'cleaners' for their apartments. But there was no mercy when it came to the death rota with women and children at the top of the list, since in their eyes they were little use as workers and contributed nothing towards the Third Reich's war effort.

The camp was suddenly crowded but the Germans had a way of making room. They would simply kill the number of people necessary to allow them to bring in the new batch of unfortunates. A few days after this latest influx, Sorge ordered everyone in the camp to line up and parade in front of him and a group of SS brought in especially from Kaiserwald.

They were looking for *Muselmänner*, a term used to describe prisoners who were too weak, too ill and too near to death to be of any use as workers, and they, along with the Hungarian women, were ordered to stand to one side, clearly surplus to requirements. They were then taken away in trucks. We never saw any of those taken away again.

We learned later that the SS in Riga had specially equipped gas trucks that put prisoners to death with the lethal gas Zyklon B, originally developed as a pesticide and then used experimentally on Soviet prisoners of war before the mass extermination of the Jews. It was also, in low doses, used as a delouser by the Germans, but in camps such as Auschwitz under Rudolf Hess, lethal quantities of Zyklon B are believed to have accounted for 1.4 million deaths. The English translation for 'Zyklon' is 'cyclone', an apt term, as that is what it was when lethal pellets were dispensed into the chambers, a cyclone of death.

It was a bad time and made worse when an engineer from Prague escaped while on a work detail. He was caught after only a couple of days and hanged on specially erected gallows in front of all of us as an example to everyone, with Sorge himself telling us we would face the same sort of execution if we tried to escape, angry that such liberties could be taken on his watch. Just to make sure no one strayed we had an X painted in yellow on the backs of our coats, our heads shaved into the shape of a cross and yellow stars emblazoned on our chests.

My gang managed to be designated to the ammunition detail near Spilve airport, moving bombs within the shelters and ferrying them from the hidden quarters to the aircraft.

Together with our small handful of Latvian Jews there were only Isidor Nussenbaum and his brother Siegfried from the German Jews, with a couple of Luftwaffe officers in charge. It was almost relaxed – well it would have been, but for the carrying of the bombs, which we were careful to keep a firm grip on.

The former German pilots and wing men were easy-going compared with the young recruits who treated us so badly and we would often engage them in conversations and arguments, which was infinitely better than moving the huge bombs around.

One day our group was arguing with the non-commissioned officers on the relative strengths of each man amongst them and our group. It resulted in the two Germans betting me that I couldn't carry one of the bombs, weighing around 500 pounds, on my back for a certain distance. The bet was for an entire carton of cigarettes, the equivalent of 200 slices of bread on the camp black market. It took several of the boys to lift the crated bomb onto my back. I staggered, at first, under the tremendous weight, but after a few stumbling steps, I found my rhythm and began walking forwards. To the guards' amazement, I carried the bomb over the line.

One thing I knew was that if the Germans struck a bet or made a promise, they would keep it and, sure enough, they reluctantly handed over the great prize, wondering how a prisoner – a Jew! – could achieve something none of the well-fed and pampered *Herrenvolk* could manage.

But such playful moments were rare breaks in the monotony of camp life and fear of the SS. One of their worst officers to pass through Latvia was Dr Rudolf Lange who moved from the Gestapo Office in Berlin to Vienna to supervise the annexation of the Austrian police and then on to Stuttgart before arriving at the Riga Ghetto with Franz Walter Stahlecker.

It is said that Lange was largely responsible for the extermination of Latvia's Jewish population and his Einsatzgruppe A commandos are reckoned to have slaughtered 250,000 in less than six months. His radical solution, totally backed by Adolf Hitler, was simply to 'kill all Jews'.

His headquarters in Riga were on Reimersa Street and he hated Jews so much he refused to look them in the eye. When one of the prisoners, Werner Koppel, was too slow in opening a door for him on a railroad car he was shot on the spot by Stahlecker. He was eventually promoted to Obersturmbannführer (Lt-Colonel), and was behind the execution of Kellerman, head of the Jewish Police at Spilve, and his thirty men.

Kellerman was the former President of the Riga Maccabi Sports Club where I boxed as a young man. He and his men were supposed to keep order amongst the Jews in the camp but, secretly, they helped the weak and the helpless.

His death, and that of his men, came after he was caught assisting a planned uprising in Riga and Spilve with stolen weapons and help from the Russian resistance. They were all executed in public as a lesson to all of us.

Sorge and Lange, who was only thirty-five when he died by his own hand, were a formidable pair, cowards who were strong only when they held guns and attack dogs to use against unarmed, half-starving prisoners. Incredibly, Sorge was not executed after the war. He became a POW under the Russians and when tried at Sachsenhausen he was convicted and sentenced to life imprisonment. Later repatriated to West Germany, he was put on trial again in Bonn and convicted of sixty-seven individual murders and many more counts of manslaughter. He finally died in Rheinbach Prison at the age of sixty-seven. I can only hope he suffered.

CHAPTER ELEVEN

THE CRUISE TO HELL (STUTTHOF)

Our unpaid labour was clearly crucial to the ever-weakening cause of the Third Reich. So much so that as the net began to tighten, with the Russians marching back into the Baltic states and driving out their old enemy, the Germans, we enslaved Jews were even transported to Germany itself. We had been moved so many times by now that it was not necessary to pack – we had long since been stripped of all personal possessions, of anything that we could call our own except our pride and will to survive. These only grew stronger, as we gathered from our gypsy-like travelling that things were not going well for Hitler's forces.

But any hope this news brought us was crushed when we learned that our destination, in occupied

Poland, was a true death camp. We were being taken to … Stutthof. If all that had gone before was a bad dream then this was the real, living nightmare for us.

We were driven from Spilve in trucks to the docks in Riga where we were marched onto a German navy ship and, weak from cold and hunger, were thrown into the very bowels of the hold. The Germans' cruelty again knew no bounds. They supplied us with no water but a large supply of salted herrings, cast down to us through a hole in the deck. They wanted us to suffer, knowing that in our hunger we would eat the fish and then have no water to slake the fierce resulting thirst.

We were in despair in our cramped quarters. Along with four Jewish boys from Helsinki I decided to break out and search for proper food and water. We knew they must have their own supplies somewhere aboard. We weighed the risks and asked ourselves, at this point, what more could they do to us? At the very worst, we'd be thrown to the fish, and then, at least, we would be out of it. It seemed there was no future, now that we were headed to a death camp … so why not take the risk?

Clearly the Germans thought we were too weak and under their thumb to try and do anything untoward, so it was quite easy for the five of us to slip out of our waterborne dungeon, climbing up the hole through which they fed us like seals and onto the main deck. After a brief search of the corridors we struck gold. We discovered a large cabin filled with packing cases and prised them open. We were dazzled to find that they had everything, the jackpot. Every case was crammed with luxurious food and alcoholic drinks. This was certainly worth risking our lives for. We took as much as we could carry down below and distributed the food and drink to everyone. There was not only canned food but also brandy, vodka and whisky, enough for everyone. If they caught us, so what? What did we care? At least we could die drunk and with full bellies. We could almost consider that a victory.

Two days later the break-in was discovered and several of us were dragged onto the deck to face the furious commanding officer. He ordered one of his men to line us up and patrol our massed rows, smelling our breath to see if we had been drinking their precious alcohol. Some of us had indeed been drinking whisky and the smell must have been noticeable, but for some reason, the sailor said nothing. No one was turned in.

They did not kill us, throw us overboard or even beat us. They simply threw us back down into the hold, took away our contraband and told us that for the next three days until we docked we would have nothing to drink and no food unless we fancied hunting rats. An armed guard was posted permanently at the entrance to our quarters.

When we docked after three days on the Baltic without sustenance we were herded into a large space with prisoners from the other boats and kept waiting for a long time as the Germans built a narrow walkway down to the dock. We soon found out why as the SS Guard lined up on each side, attacking us with clubs and the butts of their rifles as we made our way to dry land. Some prisoners fell into the water as they tried to run the gauntlet of blows raining down from both sides.

Then we were packed onto big barges like animals. Two more SS men were waiting at the entrance and another two down below, ready to continue the beating. The barges were to take us down the River Weichsel. The hatches were battened and the civilian crewmen told not to open the doors under any circumstances. It was unbearable with so many of us crammed in a small space with no food, drink or toilet facilities. Even taking a breath was difficult.

How many would have survived the three-day journey under those conditions was anyone's guess, but thanks to the humanity of the barge's civilian captain, the doors were pulled ajar to let some air in. Once we were clear of the soldiers' line of sight and fire a few of us climbed out and sat on deck, enjoying the fresh breeze. We finally docked before being force-marched for fifteen kilometres to the death camp of Stutthof. Those who could not keep up or collapsed from exhaustion were executed where they fell.

We had heard stories on the grapevine and through hidden radios of the death camps, of the gas chambers, of the mass murder of our fellow Jews. We had witnessed many horrors ourselves, losing family and friends in terrible, inhumane ways, but nothing had prepared us for what awaited in this hell hole.

We were marched through the big gates, looking in awe at the double electrified barbed wire and the guards' watchtowers, manned by soldiers with rifles, as we were pulled roughly into line, full body searched and designated our barracks.

As we arrived at our new home we were greeted by the pitiful sight of a thousand or more women and girls from Lithuania. They stood in line, heads bowed, a few loosely covered with threadbare blankets, the rest as naked as the day they were born. I only had to look at them to see that they had given up, they had lost everybody, everything, and they no longer cared what happened to them. They stood there passively, knowing they were about to die, and accepting there was no escape.

They were right. The Germans gassed every last one of them. And they called this 'war'?

It was 1944 and the camp we were in was located in the wet woodlands twenty-two miles east of Danzig. This was amongst the worst of the camps and certainly the worst I had experienced. Those who were imprisoned there did not expect to get out. There was a great deal of sickness and people dropped like flies even before they could be gassed or butchered.

It is estimated that 85,000 died at Stutthof,

equivalent to the population of a large city, but I guess the true numbers will never be known.

We watched as further thousands of women were brought in to be gassed, with only a few men amongst them. Because of the urgent need for soldiers on the front there were also a group of notorious female guards filling the vacancies as their fellow SS officers were called away. They were every bit as vicious as the worst male guards and Kapos.

The place had opened as a concentration camp in 1939 and was now a fully equipped extermination camp. The gas chambers could take up to 150 unfortunate souls at a time, with mobile gas wagons to supplement them as necessary.

It was a brutal and horrific place, where Hitler's Final Solution was implemented day by day. In addition to the gas chambers, a typhus epidemic swept through the camp in 1944, apparently the second in two years. Of course, the Germans had no inclination to nurse the sick – it was too time-consuming and expensive, when they were anyway not intended to survive. They were given injections of the lethal, rather than medicinal, variety, the Nazi's preferred means of executing children and those too weak to be taken to the ovens.

The horror stories around Stutthof were at times so horrific that even with all we had seen, it was difficult to believe them. It was rumoured that Dr Rudolf Spanner made soap from human remains, soap which was then issued to camp inmates. It was not hard to see why so many succumbed to illness in such a place, with no hope of escape and the possibility of endless torture till the end came.

As always, the only reason they kept some of us alive was their need for labourers. We were forced to slave away in twelve-hour shifts in the SS-owned businesses located near the camp; in brickyards, making armaments for the Focke-Wulf factory and working in the fields to grow their fresh vegetables.

Every morning we would be woken up with the dawn and forced to parade outside, shoes or no shoes, in rain, sun or snow. We were given a cup of 'coffee', not recognisable then or now as coffee, just a warm dark liquid with an acrid foul taste, and a piece of bread between four of us. That was our ration for the entire day.

We were fed just enough to keep us working and we were regularly deloused in huge open sheds with small amounts of Zyklon B. Each trip to the showers was potentially the last, for two pipes protruded from the walls: one poured water, while the other carried lethal doses of the deadly gas. The Nazis told us to strip naked and as we walked through the showers, we never knew what awaited us, water or poisoned gas, until the taps were turned on and water streamed down. Every drop of water felt like a reprieve.

Stutthof was a massive camp, housing not just Jews but Russians, Poles and other prisoners from the territories occupied by Germany. When the camp was liberated in May 1945, there were inmates from over twenty-five countries. Security was tight and just a touch of the electrified fence that surrounded the camp would kill.

Our barracks were filled with workers, and as we were needed for the German war effort, we were not targeted for beatings and torture or random execution as often as some of our fellow inmates. Still, the barracks were a long way from being comfortable. Between fifty and seventy of us were housed in a space that was big enough for no more than thirty. We had to share oversized beds made from rough wood without mattresses, just old clothes and straw scattered over the planks. Sleeping on such a surface left our whole bodies itching.

But there was the simple choice once more: daily pain and itchy straw or a coffin. Life was horrible but straw was always the better choice to me.

I once, in a moment of bravery, asked one of the German guards why they hated us so much. These men had the authority to do to us whatever they wanted, even down to killing without questions or reprisals. He couldn't or wouldn't answer me, and I wonder if he even knew. But at least they needed to keep the fittest alive to work for them and I remained a hard worker. Work hard or you would soon be a dark cloud coming out of a chimney, was my philosophy. There would be no compassion from our captors.

We lived every minute in fear for our lives. If a

German walked by and didn't like the look of you he would beat you on the spot, and if you limped on the way to work they simply put a gun to your head. Some gave up the ghost and died, feeling they had nothing left to live for. But I wanted to stay alive, to see my father again and find out what had happened to my brothers. That was all that I had left, the one thing that kept me going.

It was a constant war of nerves. Their sadism was never-ending; the guards and SS did everything they could to undermine our self-respect, even our sense of self, telling us we were nothing but worthless garbage and that we would die when we'd outlived our usefulness.

Hundreds of thousands died in that camp. They put the condemned in the gas chambers and then took the corpses out the other side and burned them: there were now too many bodies to bother with mass graves. But the Nazis were also trying to cover their tracks – without bodies, there would be no evidence of the slaughter beyond a few charred bones, and though they did not speak of it, many of them knew by then that the war was lost already. They had killed too many to conceal their crimes, yet they made the effort, no doubt in the hope of avoiding war crimes charges following an Allied victory.

Death camp or not, nothing was going to change either my attitude or my endless quest for food. The hunt for food to supplement our rations once more became my sole focus, the ritual that gave some meaning to my daily life.

In Stutthof, the pigs were treated better than the prisoners and certainly fed a more generous diet. When supply trains arrived at our camp, one of my jobs was to unload food for the pigs. One day an entire trainload came in, big round vegetables that looked like melons but were probably some sort of swede or pumpkin. They were fresh, untouched by mould, and I figured that if they were good enough for pigs to eat, they were certainly good enough for us.

I asked one of our guys to keep watch and to let me and a couple of the others searching the wagons know if anyone approached. It was four o'clock in the winter afternoon and already getting dark as we broke open the seals on three of the wagons, instead of just the one we were supposed to unload. We climbed into one of the cars and filled all our pockets with these large, round vegetables.

Then I heard shots and froze. I didn't know what was going on because I had heard nothing from our lookout, who was supposed to call out our code word if there looked to be trouble of any sort.

I quietly moved open the sliding doors only to see the poor guy from the next car, hanging over the side, covered in blood where he had been hit by a dum-dum bullet. His corpse was a mess, as the dum-dums exploded on impact, killing quickly and defiling the body.

I was trapped, with no idea what to do. I decided the

only course of action was to wait it out and see what happened, hardly daring to breathe as two SS men walked right up to the railway car where I hid in the furthest, darkest corner behind the piles of vegetables.

They came to a halt only inches away from where I crouched, chatting and smoking. They told their stories, finished their cigarettes, picked up their rifles and then walked away. They had missed me!

I opened up the door again and crept out into the dark. Once I had put some distance between them and myself I ran back to the barracks, blessing my luck. I was not only safe but had managed to keep hold of the food I had stolen.

Still full of adrenalin, I was frightened, shaking and very, very angry, demanding to know why our lookout hadn't called out to warn me as we'd planned. He told me he had seen the Germans at the last moment and watched as they killed one, then two, then three and finally eleven of our compatriots and he was too afraid to cry out in case they heard and shot him too. He had escaped back to our barracks.

I sat down and pulled out the precious food, keeping half for myself and giving the rest away to those who needed it most. Staying angry did no one any good. He had simply done what we were all trying to do – stay alive – and who could blame him for keeping silent? The gunshots were, after all, enough of a warning, though they came a little late.

I was, I believe, seen as something of a leader by

the weaker inmates who I fed and helped to stay alive – but this, of course, made me an object of envy to others, and a target for those who would steal from their own. I went to sleep that night with my precious vegetables stuffed in the straw mattress, but awoke in the night, feeling movement beneath me. I quickly realised that one of my fellow inmates was clawing at my bed to get to my food. I waited until I knew his hand was inside my mattress and then I grabbed it, holding it fast.

For the second time in one day I was angry not with the Germans, but a fellow prisoner and said, 'I gave you and the others half my food. Why did you come to me to rob me now, after I risked my life for you?'

He shivered with fear and said nothing

'Why did you do it?' I demanded again.

'I was hungry,' was his only reply. I pushed him away. How could I remain angry? I knew, all too well, the risks that hunger could drive a man to take: I took them almost every day myself.

Sadly that sort of thing happened to me many times. Some inmates didn't have the guts to go out amongst the Germans and steal for themselves, so they took from those of us willing to face the danger. These thefts hurt, because I always shared my bounty a widely as I could. There was little they could give me in return, although they knew I would always give away my best food for a pair of well soled and heeled shoes or boots. Damaged and infected feet were a massive and untreated problem in the concentration camps. Good shoes and good socks remained important to survive the long workdays and there were always those who were more than willing to exchange them for dinner.

This concentration camp was vastly different from anything I had experienced before. There were no such recreational activities as boxing, football or even time to exercise. Breathing was the only luxury. Even stolen food was harder to come by and my weight dropped alarmingly. It was every man for himself and the eclectic mix of inmates – Jews, Russians, Poles, the fiercely independent Gypsies – produced its share of collaborators. I'm afraid that amongst our own Jewish people, there were those who would do almost anything to cling to what little life they had left.

I had my brushes with the seedier elements in the barracks. There was one Polish collaborator in particular who became my Stutthof nemesis. He was tall and as mean as a dog with two heads, and continually beat up my little friend Osha, whom I had kept under my wing since rescuing him in Riga. Naturally I did what I could to protect Osha and I fought the Pole on a regular basis until I was caught by the guards. They dragged me in front of Obersturmbannführer Werner Hoppe, the commandant of the Stutthof camp and a very twisted individual.

Hoppe had been invalided out of the army with

a severe leg wound when fighting the Red Army in Novograd in 1942. He retrained in Auschwitz where he impressed the SS with his cruelty and was promoted to Kommandant of Stutthof. He was also in charge at the Wöbbelin transition camp before being arrested by the British in Holstein in 1946.

He struck me once, twice, called me a damned Jew and worse and demanded to know why I had attacked the Pole. I explained it was because the man was always beating up my little brother. He told me he wasn't going to let me get away with it and sentenced me to twenty-five lashes. I was, he told the SS guards, to count each lash out loud as they beat me, and if I missed a single one, they were to start again from zero.

The guards took me out to the yard, stripped me and paraded me in front of all the prisoners both to humiliate and to make an example of me. The SS man used their traditional punishment rod, made of flexible steel and covered in rubber to beat me and I soon began to lose count in a haze of pain.

My vision blurred as the rod struck and I gasped for breath, trying to keep count of the lashes. But the searing pain of each blow brought me close to losing consciousness, and I missed count several times. I was out of my mind. I didn't know who I was or where I was. I couldn't walk because I was so swollen. I didn't even see the guy who beat me because I had my front to the wall and I eventually passed out. I later learned that I had suffered eighty lashes of the whip and was clearly fortunate not to have suffered permanent damage – or worse!

I was swollen, blue, black and green with bruises running from my neck to my ankles, when the beating finally ceased. They threw me down the steps like a lump of meat into the basement where I lay in agony. The guards casually walked away, talking between themselves as if they had just been out for a stroll.

I am sure that but for the fitness and strength of character given to me by my chosen sport I would have died that day. The pain was indescribable. I slept there overnight and although the guards were surprised to discover me still breathing the next morning I was dragged out and sent back to my duties at the airport. There was no choice and I knew the penalty for disobedience or failure to keep the pace demanded by our masters. I went back to my search for food.

One of the advantages of being young, fit and relatively strong was that we were assigned to all sorts of work details, some of them taking us into the city. Groups of us would go out in trucks and we had a chance to meet other people, normal people who were going about their lives beyond the world of concentration camps and Ghettos. But they were also prisoners of a kind, Poles who had become Germans overnight, living under occupation since the war's early days. Some even had sympathy for us. The guards would leave us with civilians while they went off to drink, smoke and chase girls, and it was always a relief to be under such comparatively gentle scrutiny.

Most of the Poles we came into contact with were not much better than the Latvians when it came to anti-Semitism, but they were easy to barter with, and happy to do deals with us. A Pole or two might have thought themselves the winner of negotiations when I exchanged vodka for good boots – but I knew well which was more useful for surviving in the camp.

CHAPTER TWELVE

MAGDEBURG AND LIBERATION

It seemed no Jew would leave Stutthof alive, no matter what the outcome of the war, and I had almost resigned myself to death in the camp from which it seemed impossible to escape. Then, suddenly, there was a glimpse of salvation. The Germans, ever desperate to prop up their fading war effort, needed men and asked for engineers to go outside the camp to work. I volunteered and lied my way through the interviews, despite my lack of any engineering background. Once more I was on my way again, out of the awful death camp.

My lies paid handsome dividends. I was transported by train to Magdeburg, more of a labour camp than a death camp, a place where death was only likely rather than guaranteed! But with the war slipping away from the Germans, there was another concern, what was going to happen to the prisoners, particularly the

Jews, who had witnessed so many war crimes, murders and executions, when the Allies arrived? Would we be allowed to survive even if the Americans, the British or the Russians came to liberate the innocent as their three-pronged attack began to take its toll?

There was, however, no time to think of such things. Survival and hunger were still all that mattered and it would not do to let the mind wonder about what might lie ahead, though I knew the day of reckoning was coming ever closer. Rumours abounded that both the Russians and the Americans were heading towards Magdeburg and we managed to get snippets of news from an illicit radio and the usual gossip in the factories.

In the Magdeburg camp there was an officer in charge of a small section, someone we thought of as a real Nazi and a Jew-hater, who kept an eye on about a dozen of us. He had me cleaning up the grease and the oil in the pit below the anti-aircraft guns. A strange job for an alleged engineer, but at least it meant I wasn't exposed as a liar.

One day I went down into the pit and began clearing up when I saw a piece of white paper. I was inquisitive, as usual, and when I looked I discovered what was left of a ham sandwich wrapped in the paper. I didn't stop to look for the Nazi to ask if he had finished with what was clearly his breakfast. I just ate it. When he returned from whatever he had been doing he said to me: 'What have you done with my breakfast, you fucking Jew?'

I held his hard look and said: 'I worked hard, did what you asked me and I ate the sandwich because it was left over and I was hungry.'

I feared for the worse when he launched a kick at my arse, but as he was doing it I caught the hint of a smile on his face. From then on, whenever I worked under his supervision he deliberately left me a sandwich to find.

Was this kindness on his part or just another brand of sadism? You are hungry, working for slops and stale bread, eat what real food is discarded and then get your ass kicked anyway. The sandwich is there, but not for you. Or is it? He brought the food for me every day, but always made me pay for eating it. Even what little kindness such guards sometimes showed was laced with humiliation, asserting their superiority. But I wasn't about to argue the point.

We were housed in the old Magdeburg barracks previously used by the Polish soldiers, a slight improvement on the conditions we had faced in Stutthof. Daily life remained a nightmare of exhaustion. We were there to work, and that is what we did for hour after hour, unloading trainloads of coal with just shovels. There were also a number of munitions factories and other war-related plants where we worked anything up to eighteen hours at a stretch, according to what had been given priority that day. I cannot imagine why they wanted engineers for this purely manual work.

Again, my fitness helped and I was even able to help some of those who couldn't keep the pace. The price of sickness or injury was still death; a sick Jew was of no use to the Germans.

We were given the day off on Sundays – but not so that you would notice. There was no work as such but, instead, we had to clean the barracks and the toilets and clear the tables after the Germans had eaten. Once again we were on a lower level than slaves.

Gradually news began to filter through the grapevine that the Americans were moving ever closer and the Germans decided that they were going to take us on a forced march to Lake Elbe, presumably to kill us and bury the evidence beneath the water. By this point, the Germans were taking many thousands of Jews and dissidents on Death Marches throughout Europe and we were earmarked for one of these journeys to nowhere.

One of the German soldiers asked me who I thought was going to win the war. I told him he didn't need to ask me because he already knew the answer, and that was why they were preparing to move us out of Magdeburg. He became very threatening, called me a son-of-a-bitch and threatened to kill me. I just shrugged and told him his countrymen had already killed everyone I held dear and he didn't frighten me. He stalked off, furious. It was clear now that their time was coming, and I suspect he didn't shoot me because he realised I had told him the truth.

Yet while we all knew now that Germany would lose the war, we were in no way safer than before. The Russians and British bombed the city day and night. I was run down by the years of hard work, inadequate food and torture. My knees hurt badly and I was constantly depressed. I had only lasted this long because I had been young and strong when war began and I was first imprisoned. Now I was reaching the end of my strength. I wasn't sure how much longer I could hold out and whether the war would end before I gave up my last breath.

The Germans were putting up a stout defence. As the 30th US Infantry Division drew near, the German Commanding General Regener not only refused to surrender but declined to even talk to the Americans. Left with no alternative, the Americans pounded Magdeburg with artillery and air raids on 16 April for twenty-four hours, finally forcing the Germans to surrender.

We heard the sirens wail out their warning and we started to run, looking for shelter from the deadly rain. At first the Germans wouldn't let us into the air raid shelters, but common sense prevailed when they realised they would need us after the bombing stopped to clear up the mess. Many hundreds of people died during the intense bombing of Magdeburg on that day, wiping out the old city centre and reducing vast numbers of buildings to rubble.

The bombers targeted the factories of Krupp-Gruson Werk, the Junkerswerk and the Brabag, where many of us worked, forcing everyone to flee to the suburbs while trains were deployed to carry children and the sick out of the city. Many of the prisoners were herded into the Neue Welt Stadium as artillery shells continued to pour down on the besieged city and there was total panic when two grenades or shells exploded in the stadium. Naturally the prisoners tried to escape, only to be fired upon by SS men with machine guns waiting outside.

The Germans had used Magdeburg as a showpiece prison, filming while they entertained the Red Cross. It was, of course, all false, and no sooner had the Red Cross officials departed than everything returned to normal. They didn't witness the old and the sick. They didn't see the many dying Jews or the storerooms where they kept the goods stolen from the Jews when they arrived. It was all a sham. In fact the Americans uncovered vast amounts of treasure and currency hidden in Magdeburg.

My end almost came sooner than I expected. As the front approached Magdeburg we discovered from our illicit radio that prisoners of war should gather at set points so they would be safe from attack when the Americans finally roared into the city.

The Germans were in disarray. We had to escape

the camp to avoid a massacre from either friend or foe and the only way out was over the electrified fence that surrounded our quarters. I was second in the line and watched as the man in front went over without any trouble but when I tried my hand snagged on the electrical wire, sparks began to fly and I could smell burning flesh as my hand was held firm by the electric current crashing through my body.

I was as weak as I had ever been during those long years as a prisoner and I was not going to survive this trauma for long. But once more my luck held firm. The man who had gone before me was, incredibly, an electrician and knew exactly what to do. He saved my life, grabbing a piece of scrap iron and throwing it with perfect aim at the electric wire, causing it to short. I fell to the ground, electrocuted and close to death. All I could think of was I had survived so much and here I was about to die with the end of the war just around the corner.

The other prisoners dragged me into a huge sewer pipe where we hid until some German civilians from one of the factories where we had been made to work found us. They told us everything was almost over and there was a free clinic for any of the sick to attend. They were partly right. It was as good as over but a small band of Germans were still holding on.

Did we believe them or was this a trap? I had no choice. It was either trust or die. I reported to the clinic with considerable help and they promptly buried me up to my neck in the earth to neutralise the effects of the electricity. My paranoia was running berserk and I thought I was going to be literally buried alive, but it turned out to be an effective treatment. I couldn't walk when they pulled me out so they did it all over again, pushing me into a hole and shovelling earth on me. This time it worked and I regained some of the use of my limbs. I was very weak and walking was difficult but gradually I recovered enough strength to be taken back to the basement of the factory where we were working at the time, this time to unload a trainload of potatoes for the remnants of the German army.

After unloading them they all had to be put in sacks ready for the retreating Germans. We worked there hour after hour until every potato had been put in a sack. We took a well-earned rest, watched over by a Romanian SS man who sat smoking his pipe when, suddenly, the air raid sirens started to wail yet again. The Romanian just laughed and said that we damned Jews would be killed where we worked by the people who were trying to liberate us. It was a provocation too far and one of our guys knocked him out with a piece of wood. We stripped him of his clothes and found that both his boots and trousers were more or less my size. I put them on. Why not? I was not shy. He would happily have seen us dead, and we at least left him alive.

I led the three other Jews out into the street, acting as though I was a German taking them back to camp.

We had to be careful because we wanted to run neither into the Germans who would quickly expose us, nor the Russians who had already been in and out of the city and would have killed us as soon as look at us.

I took them to the basement of another factory I knew where, at one stage, we were forced to make anti-aircraft shells for the German guns. I remembered there was a maze of rooms and corridors down there and it provided a safe hiding place until the Americans arrived later that same day.

The SS had fled in the face of the superior force rolling into the city and all was chaos. No one knew who was who as uniforms were discarded and civilian clothes adopted.

When our lookouts realised it was the Americans coming through we made enough noise for them to know we were down in the cellars. We didn't want to go outside to expose ourselves and be shot down by mistake. They too were understandably cautious and called down that if there were any Germans they were to come out with their hands in the air. We stayed quiet and still until they called out for anyone from the concentration camp to come out. That was our signal and up we came, very slowly and very carefully with our hands high in the air.

There was just one problem. I was still wearing the borrowed SS clothes liberated from the Romanian and had, in the moment of excitement of freedom, forgotten to remove them. I was called to a halt and told to put my hands on my head. The Americans clearly thought I was a German and told me so. Nothing I said could persuade them otherwise and they were not prepared to listen to a man in a black uniform even if my fellow prisoners were backing up my claims.

I was made to wait in silence until a Jewish soldier in an American colonel's uniform arrived. Once apprised of the situation, he started reading a prayer from the Jewish bible and told me to finish it off – in Hebrew!

I was seriously out of practice but it was no problem. The prayer, the *Shema Yisrael*, was ingrained deep in my mind, and I trembled with emotion as I spoke the ancient words. I was finally accepted for what I was and we were taken out. What an irony it would have been if I had travelled all that distance, suffered for so long, only to have been imprisoned or worse, by the very people who had come to save us. But we were liberated and I was still alive.

The Americans were stunned by what they found, particularly the sheer number of prisoners as they stumbled across a slave labour camp which held American and British POWs as well as our large contingent of Jews spread around the city and the camps. The 743rd Tank Battalion discovered a train crowded with 2,400 political prisoners, men, women and children, most of them Jews and all of them sick and weakened after days stranded on the stationary train without food, water or sanitary facilities.

With the Russians moving towards the east of the city on the other side of the Elbe River, the Americans, uncertain how they would react to us, moved many freed prisoners in a fleet of trucks, putting us up in the now empty Luftwaffe Barracks and demanding the local German civilian population should provide us with proper food.

We were taken away and given fresh clothing but not that much to eat. I was baffled and annoyed until it was gently explained to us that we had been starved and maltreated to the point that our stomachs had shrunk to such an extent that they could digest very little. A number of those liberated from the camps died from such an 'overdose', digging their own graves with knives and forks.

But I was ready to eat. I had spent the past five years risking my life stealing scraps of food fit only to be thrown away in normal times to stay alive. I had gone through grim times, learning to eat anything in order to survive. Some of the things I swallowed, insects and rodents, I would not repeat and I never told my children just how low I sank at times. Now good food, real food was available for nothing, with no need to steal and fear the consequences, yet still they would not let me eat.

We were liberated but I had no feelings of relief or anything else. Many of us felt dead inside after all the suffering we had seen and all that we had gone through. We were little more than empty shells, stumbling in a state of shock. Too much thinking would bring back too many bad memories, too many things that were consigned to nightmares and not waking hours.

My legs were giving me the biggest problem and they gave me injections and took me to hospital where I was told I would have to stay for a few days while they kept an eye on me.

On reflection their decision probably kept me alive because I would have eaten whatever I could have got my hands on. But they were wise and took their time building up both my rations and my strength. Before long, I was on my feet again and blessed to have survived.

When I was discharged the Jewish colonel who had tested my Hebrew by way of determining my true identity and a Christian colonel summoned me to their office to quiz me about what had happened, asking exactly what we had gone through. They wanted to know if I could remember and recognise any or all of the SS officers who worked in the factory and in the camp and whether I could point them out.

Of course I could! These bastards' faces were imprinted on my mind and as we drove around the ruins of Magdeburg and Hillersleben I recognised and pointed out one after another, disguised as civilians. They rounded up every one of them and during that time I built up a strong rapport and a lasting friendship with the two American colonels, especially Dave Topolski, the man I had joined in prayer.

Two of the commandants of the Magdeburg Camp, Karl Rahm and Siegfried Seidl, were tried in courts in Litoměřice and Vienna and then executed. Rahm was in charge when I arrived, handing over the camp to the Red Cross before making his escape. He was caught in Austria and charged with crimes against humanity and his part in murdering Jews in Auschwitz before his arrival in Magdeburg.

Freedom after long years of oppression is a strange, almost magical feeling – made all the more unreal, for us, as we were still amongst the people who for years had killed our friends and families and tortured us. We had no money or possessions but we were alive and free and we painted the town red in our own fashion. I led the way, telling the others the Germans had taken away what we had so they, at least, could stand us a few free meals and drinks. They owed us that and a lot more.

There was not much left of Magdeburg beyond rubble but just fourteen miles away was the town of Hillersleben, which had escaped that sort of damage. After visiting the local restaurants, asking for the hospitality the Americans had promised we would receive, I led our group to the home of the Mayor of Hillersleben. He lived in a beautiful house undamaged by the war. I strode up to the front door, hammered on the ornate knocker and demanded to see the Mayor.

When he arrived, with fear etched into his face, I told him we had nowhere to sleep and we would like to stay with him for a night or two and join him for something to eat. He slammed the door in my face. That was a mistake. I broke the door down and told him we were coming in anyway. He then made another mistake when he tried to physically eject me. I took hold of him and with five years of pent up anger bubbling up inside me, I told him the Nazis had pushed me around for too long, and promptly threw him down the stairs. Those who had oppressed us were armed: the Mayor was not, and I told him if he didn't leave with his family at once I would remove him forcefully. He took one look at my face and saw that I was deadly serious. He gathered his frightened family together and left.

I was on firm ground because the Americans had explicitly told us to go out and enjoy ourselves and do what we wanted, anything we wanted short of murder and rape. They promised they wouldn't take any action against us for anything we did for forty-eight hours.

They did so knowing only too well what depriva- tion we had suffered for so long and they understood what sorts of things would happen once we were let loose. The Americans had as much sympathy for the Germans as we did; they had lost friends and comrades and seen the devastation and suffering in the concentration camps they had liberated.

So the Mayor became a refugee and we moved into

his thirty-bedroom mansion. The numbers were just about right, as I had gathered together a group of around sixty people.

Having found a place to stay, we then needed to ensure there was enough food for the next few days and our search took us down into the cellars where we found another of those veritable German treasure troves. There were whole pigs hanging from the ceiling next to half a cow, smoked ham, the sort of things we could only dream about. Can you imagine how we felt? There were racks of fine wines, champagne, crates of beer, and cases of brandy. These things had been beyond our dreams even in the best of times.

We had quite a party that night.

The Americans were desperately keen to do the right thing by the survivors and they told me they had arranged for us all to move into a transit camp, the old Luftwaffe billets. Just the word 'camp' was enough for me to refuse, passionately. We had had enough of Ghettos, labour camps, concentration camps, and any sort of camp carried with it bad vibrations.

By this time I had been elected unofficial leader of the refugees and when I said no, several hundred of my followers said no as well and, instead, we found ourselves quartered in commandeered apartments in Hillersleben.

They might have been the liberating army but we had all had enough of camps and we were in such a state of mind that we trusted no one but each other and were frightened of what else might lie in store for us. We were also told that the Russians would like us to go 'home'. What an irony that was! I had grown up with the Latvian gentiles and the Russians telling us to go home, to leave their country and find our own. Now, because they had lost so many men in the war, they needed us to fill the gaps and work for the state. It sounded like something I had heard before!

The Americans understood the situation only too well and told us that although we would have to meet the Russians and listen to them we could make up our own minds and do what we wanted to do and they would back us to the hilt. The Russians, who were swarming all over the east of the country and heading for Berlin, drove in to meet us in a big convoy of cars and trucks, roaring up to the designated meeting place, their red flag flying. They had brought with them clothes for us and sent important colonels to tell us what to do.

As a Russian speaker I was nominated to translate for these men, who had come straight from the front. I took an instant dislike to them; they were too much like the Germans – killers! You could almost smell it on them.

The first thing they asked me when they knew I was from Latvia was why I and the others were not already back in Riga now that the war was over. I told them it was because they, the Russians, had told us Jews to go to Palestine before the war when they were drunk or mad or on the rampage. I told them we were not going back to Russia or Latvia: we were taking their good advice and going to Palestine where we belonged.

The General in charge of the Russian delegation – he never did give me his calling card – was infuriated by my little speech and leapt to his feet with his face as red as the flag on his uniform, threatening me.

How could this pompous arrogant man think he could frighten me after all I had been through? I laughed at him and told him that after being in concentration camps for so long my nerves would barely feel another beating, and that nothing he could do would frighten me.

He wouldn't relent, and snapped back that they had clothes for us to put on and trucks to take us back to Russia. That was the end of the matter as far as he was concerned.

My friend the American colonel had been listening quietly to our exchange and asked our group if we were willing to go to Russia with the General. I told him that my answer was a definite 'no', but I would not speak for the others. They were requested to stand to the left if they wanted to go to Russia and to the right if they preferred to take their chances in Palestine.

Everyone moved to their right and I turned to the Russian General, thanked him, and said we would see him in Palestine. With that I walked away.

The furious and defeated Russians stormed into their cars and trucks and roared off into the distance, a plume of dust trailing behind them. A sight I will never forget.

CHAPTER THIRTEEN

THE PATH TO PALESTINE

The fighting may have stopped, but the war, so far as my friends and I were concerned, was far from over. Our private battle continued. We were homeless, without money and with nowhere to go. Our dream was to have a home of our own in a land of our own, to travel to Palestine and help establish a Jewish nation in our own country.

The logistics of making this dream come true were problematic, what with no money, no transport, no influence and few who were willing to help. Obviously, staying in Germany for a moment longer than we had to was out of the question, while Latvia was not an option for me at least, as I did not view the Russians or the Latvians as very different from the Germans. Why escape Hitler's boot only to be crushed by Stalin's heel?

There was, as far as I knew, no longer any family for

me to return to in Latvia. I still hoped and believed that my father Mordechai was in Palestine and I was determined to find him.

All I and my group wanted was to be allowed to leave the German soil we despised. A simple request, on the face of it, and little enough to ask after all we had been put through with so much of the world turning their backs on us and failing to recognise the genocide happening under their noses. But there was no parting of the waters, no smooth passage for me to meet my long-lost father, only more torment and huge obstacles that tried my patience to the very limit.

I led a group of survivors to the Zionist organisations who were helping their fellow Jews head for the Promised Land and I was told, to my delight, those with relatives already in Palestine would be given priority and first option. But after I attended my one-on-one interview I saw that my application was placed at the bottom of the pile instead of the top. I wanted to know why and what was happening but I was hurried away and told I would be given an explanation later.

It transpired that as a known Beitar supporter, I belonged to the wrong political group, the right wing, and I would have to seek them out if I were to be taken to Palestine. Had I survived through a war and death camps only to be denied a place in my rightful homeland due to my politics? I was astonished that my fellow Jews would refuse to help me over

political factionalism, but the left was then domi-
nant in the Zionist movement, and they clearly had
their priorities.

Still, I was determined I would make it one way
or another. The group I had gathered around me had
swollen to around 1,000 and I led an exodus of Jews
from the ruined city of Magdeburg, heading for the
Belgian port of Antwerp. It was a large unwieldy
group but I had friends amongst the Americans who
made sure we were supplied with a train to take us on
the first leg of our journey out of Europe.

Trains were not our favourite mode of transport
after some of the experiences we had suffered but this
time we were able to sit in real carriages and proper
seats, rather than suffocating in cattle trucks en route
to the concentration camps or the gas chambers.

The anger of our suffering and the problems we
were facing as we fought to start new lives in our
chosen home came boiling to the surface on that
train ride. This particular group of people had been
pushed to the limits and beyond and now the anger
they had been forced to suppress erupted. At almost
every German station we passed through on the way
to Belgium we left a trail of destruction. We were
like a group of ill-behaved teenagers. We would pull
the communication cord to halt the train at random
stations, jump out and abuse any Germans standing
on the platforms.

Eventually the American Military Policemen who

were following us had enough and told us if we continued in that fashion they would turn the train around and take us straight back to Magdeburg. We ignored them, not believing they would carry out their threat but they proved to be as good as their word. The next time we laid siege to a station we were hustled back onto the train and taken straight back to Magdeburg. The Americans were still sympathetic and didn't want to imprison us or keep us in the German city for any length of time and eventually we promised to behave, under the threat of criminal charges for any misdemeanours, and off we went again.

We arrived first of all in the Belgian city of Charleroi where the local Jewish community, warned in advance of our arrival, had arranged empty buildings for us to use as temporary accommodation with two or three of us to a room. There were also kitchens in each of the buildings but I kept away from them and soon started trading whatever I could so that we could eat out at restaurants in the city, a real luxury.

For all our bravado it took us a while, however, to gather enough courage to go out and about like normal people. We were still looking over our shoulders and waiting for soldiers to scream instructions at us or beat us with the butts of their guns or truncheons.

We saw anyone in a uniform as a potential threat as we struggled to accept the war was over and regain our status as civilised human beings.

There was time to adjust for we were in Charleroi

for some months while the lengthy arrangements were made to move us on. Undoubtedly, we were a very difficult and embarrassing group of people to handle. The world had, by and large, ignored us as the Germans dehumanised and slaughtered us. Churchill is said to have admitted that saving Jewish lives was not a war priority, although it should not have been too difficult to bomb the train lines taking Jews into the camps and chambers.

It gave us all time to think and reflect. More than sixty years on I still have nightmares when we talk and reminisce about those horrendous days – so imagine how it was then, while it was all still fresh in our minds. It was hard to sleep and when we did there was little relief for the nightmares would come as soon as our eyes closed. For some the bad dreams simply never went away, waking or sleeping. Such an endless mental onslaught claimed the lives of some weakened survivors who simply could not take it. We were afraid of everything, anyone knocking on the door, day or night, a wrong look in the street or even raised voices.

Take someone out of a normal prison and put him on the streets after five or ten years inside and he will be lost, for a while, as he struggles to adjust to freedom. Add to that all the cruelty we had suffered and everything else we went through and you can see how frightening and wonderful it was to walk those streets as free men. There was so much anger and bitterness, we had all lost most of our families and friends, and our youth had been taken away from us along with our freedom. It was impossible not to think about what might have been. I was sure that I could have gone far as a boxer because I was strong for my size, quick on my feet and I knew how to finish a fight with a clean knockout. But that was all in the past and could never be recovered.

What was I to do? I still felt isolated and unwanted. My plight remained unresolved. I had no ticket for the boat and no papers to get me into British-occupied Palestine.

Then I remembered my friend, the Jewish American colonel, David Topolski. I tracked him down through the American offices in the city and to my delight discovered, by a stroke of good fortune, that he was close by, still keeping an eye on his ill-behaved friends. After I had pointed out the Nazis in Magdeburg he had promised that if ever he could help in any way he would. When I told him of my plight he was as good as his word. He did not hesitate. He jumped to his feet, took me outside and told me to climb into his jeep.

He drove me straight to the American quartermaster's stores and, pulling rank, provided me with a full American soldier's uniform, complete with an army kitbag for my few personal possessions. There I was with smart, new clothes that actually fitted me and, of course, good, solid, well-made boots. Things were definitely looking up.

Next stop was an office where he again used his rank and his contacts to somehow obtain a pass confirming that I was what my uniform suggested, an American soldier given leave to take a vacation in Palestine. He then personally drove me to the port and accompanied me up the gangplank of a waiting ship, where my pass was accepted by the guards on duty and I was allowed on board. Only then did my colonel salute, turn his back and walk away. However, typically, my troubles were not over. One of the left-wingers from the other side of the Jewish political divide recognised me and told the ship's captain I was a fake and shouldn't be allowed to sail. The captain was left with little option but to investigate how I came to be on board.

I showed him my pass and pointed to the retreating colonel, asking him if he wanted me to call him back to verify my claims. He shook his head and turned on the man who had reported me, telling him to mind his own business and to keep out of his way for the rest of the trip. After so many aborted attempts I was finally on my way to the Promised Land and, hopefully, to the long awaited reunion with my father, if he was still alive and I could find him. The thought of this reunion had driven me on in the darkest hours, forcing me to cling to hope and life. I wasn't going to give up now.

But, true to form, nothing was ever going to be easy. The problem remained, I had no papers to permit me to even disembark and it wouldn't take a genius to see through my disguise as an American soldier, never mind settle in the country of my choice. If I and the others who were entering the country illegally walked down the gangplank the occupying British – rigidly enforcing their policy of restricting the number of immigrants permitted to enter Palestine – would immediately put us into a detention camp. That word again.

Desperate times need desperate measures. So nothing new there! At least I was on my way to Palestine, and after the long sea journey we arrived at the Port of Haifa. The dockside was thronged with people waiting to greet friends and relatives. But there were many of us on board who couldn't simply walk down the gangplank. Almost half the passengers on board that ship were not legally entitled to enter Palestine.

There was nothing for it but to jump from the deck of this big ocean-going liner into the water and swim for shore. It was dangerous, even amidst the general chaos that accompanies a docking liner, as it was a long fall into the water and there was a British military station and soldiers close by.

But arrangements for us had secretly been made ahead by radio as we took advantage of the fading light and the usual hustle and bustle on the dockside. Our allies on the beach guided us in with their lights.

Fortunately I had been a swimmer all my life and, incredibly, we all made it to the beach without problems, unnoticed by the British. We were taken to a strategically placed kibbutz (communal settlement) near Haifa where we changed out of our wet clothes, showered, had dinner and a good night's sleep.

Dawn brought more obstacles because of my political leanings. The group who had fished us out of the water told me I couldn't remain there because theirs was a left-wing settlement and our political beliefs clashed. I told them about my father, and asked if they could help me find him, and although it seemed the political overrode all other considerations – they were left, I was right – to my great joy they gave me the news I was desperate to hear: not only was my father still alive but they also knew he lived somewhere in Tel Aviv. Furthermore, they had the good grace to give me the bus fare to go into Tel Aviv. It was a Jewish holiday and no Jewish buses were running, so I happily caught the local Arab bus into town.

From the information I had been given, I roughly knew the neighbourhood where he lived and started asking people if they knew a man named Shapov, the name we used until we went to America. Eventually someone said they knew him and would take me to where he lived.

I realised I was holding my breath as I followed this man and suddenly there he was. My father. It was all very emotional. We hugged each other for the first time in eleven years. Was that all it was! Until that moment he had not known whether I was dead or alive, he didn't even know officially that his wife was dead or what had happened to my brothers.

There is a Jewish law, I was told, stating that when you are overseas for a decade and you don't know what has happened to your family, whether they are alive or dead, you are allowed to remarry. This is what he had done and I discovered that far from being alone with my father I now had a little half-brother named Simon and a stepmother, Sarah, a really nice lady. She was originally from Lithuania, almost a neighbour as it was one of our three Baltic states.

That night I sat under the sky eating dinner with my father when I heard automatic machine-gun fire. I was stunned because I knew the British had banned all private weapons and I asked my father what was going on. He explained that the country was in turmoil. Since the 1920s, spurred on by the Grand Mufti of Jerusalem (a puppet of Mussolini and Hitler, who even provided a lavish BMW and chauffeur for the Mufti's wartime visits to Berlin) there had been waves of attacks on Jewish settlements, small villages were destroyed, and many Jewish settlers murdered. The underground Jewish military organisation – the Haganah – under the control of David Ben-Gurion, did what they could, with limited resources to protect them. From time to time, the British had limited Jewish immigration to Palestine, and after the war, with survivors of the camps desperate to get to Palestine, these restrictions had become ever more severe and onerous, and attempts to escape the British blockade by refugees, packed into rickety ships, ever more desperate.

The Jews, therefore, found themselves confronted by two enemies, as they saw it – the British, who were far from even-handed in their dealings with the two sides, and the militant Arabs. Through all this, Ben-Gurion strove to steer a moderate cause and not to antagonise the British, who recognised him as the leader of the Jewish community in Palestine (the *Yishuv*). He himself had come to the country from Russia as a boy in 1906, working on the land which at that time was largely uncultivated and overrun with Malarial swamps.

However, others, myself and my father included, felt that more desperate and aggressive tactics were necessary, which is how the two extreme military groups with which I was to become involved came into being – The Irgun (under Menachem Begin) and the Stern Gang (under the leadership of the young Hebrew poet, Abraham Stern). Theirs was a philosophy and approach I could respond to, especially after the nightmare I had endured in Germany. Clearly we were dealing with people who did not play by the rules, who punched low, and I had learned how best to respond to that.

My father told me they were his 'boys' – those

belonging to the same political wing I had belonged to in Riga. Their aim was to get Palestine back from the British and create a nation-state for Jews. He told me: 'Today you are quietly eating your dinner and enjoying your freedom. Tomorrow I will take you to meet them. Be prepared because it will be very different.'

At noon the next day he took me to meet the leader of the right-wing commandos who were totally committed to establishing a Jewish State, however they had to do it. I had been a member of the same organisation from a very early age but my father warned me this time there was no dancing, no boxing, no social clubs – just fighting!

I told him the reasons why I had come to Palestine – first, to see him and secondly to join the fight for our independence. Three days later, they gave me a handgun and a rifle. The prisoner was now a soldier. It was as quick as that.

CHAPTER FOURTEEN

HELA

Perhaps the most remarkable aspect of my story is that in the midst of all the horror I found myself a lasting love, a single rose that grew and blossomed.

Hela, my wife-to-be, was a fellow concentration camp survivor, and we met during the liberation. Though I had put a figurative arm around this young girl, protecting her from the chaos, we were both still in a state of shock, and did not recognise the possibilities between us. But when we came together in Jerusalem, I knew I did not want to be parted from her ever again, and, thankfully, she shared my feelings. Here we are now, still together more than fifty years later, supporting each other on a day-to-day basis and as much in love as ever.

I was first introduced to Hela after our liberation when a mutual friend came to me and asked if I would look after a young girl. She was alone, searching

Magdeburg for survivors of her family, and would soon become lost and in despair if someone didn't keep an eye open for her. I have to confess it wasn't love at first sight. At that time there was no thought of romance, never mind marriage. But I took her under my wing, brought her in with the group and made sure she was looked after.

She joined us on our journey from Hillersleben to Magdeburg, through Holland and on into Belgium before I finally sailed to Palestine. At least, that is how I remember the central events that brought us together and to what would, in time, become the State of Israel. But my wife and mother of our children, and fellow survivor of the camps, Hela has more than earned the right to tell her own story. So here it is, in her words:

HELA'S STORY

Before the war, I lived in a beautiful little apartment in Ozorków, a small town near Łódź in Poland. When the German soldiers came, we were evicted on the spot, permitted to take only one small suitcase. I had no choice but to leave almost everything behind – clothes, jewellery, family keepsakes – and a German family moved in at gunpoint and took it all over. I was moved to the Łódź Ghetto. The Ghetto Litzmannstadt, as it was called, was the second largest in Poland and was originally intended to be a staging post for Jews in transit to the camps. But the large supply of slave labour it provided made Łódź an important industrial resource for the war effort, and the Nazis took full advantage.

Overnight, Poles we had considered friends turned on us, or simply looked away as Poland's Jews were imprisoned, killed or exiled. As with Nathan's native Latvia, Polish culture included a deep seam of historic anti-Semitism, and Stalin's part in the invasion of Poland, while still Hitler's ally, reinforced the old myth that Jews and Bolsheviks were one and the same.

There was no public outcry at the treatment of the Jews. Entire families disappeared, some dragged from their homes while in the middle of a meal, leaving their food on the dining table. The camp, by the time I was taken there, was huge and very over-crowded. At the entrance there was a sign which said: *Wohngebiet Der Juden Betreten Verboten* ('Jewish Residential Area – Entry Forbidden').

More than a third of the city's population was crammed into a small area, most of which had neither running water nor a sewage system. As a result many of the population – as much as 20 per cent – died from thirst and disease. Our daily ration of food was just ten grams of bread. Many were taken straight to the gas chambers and others were buried alive in mass graves. The remainder were expected to work as slave labour, producing uniforms for the German army.

The Ghetto survived until August 1944 because of its usefulness to the German war effort. But as the Germans realised that the war was lost, thousands, including many Roma Gypsies, were taken to the extermination camp at Chelmno, where at least 152,000 died and, according to records, only two survived. Those of us who were left were taken to the death camp of Konzentrationslager Auschwitz, a city in its own right, with a complex infrastructure of concentration and extermination camps. The camp was built by the Nazis in Polish areas they took over during the early days of the Second World War and then isolated, soldiers driving away all the local inhabitants.

It was the largest of the many German concentration camps and was built around the original Auschwitz I, the former Polish Army barracks. Auschwitz II – Birkenau – was the extermination and women's camp and Auschwitz III – Buna-Monowitz – a labour camp. Forty or more satellite camps dotted the surrounding countryside.

Auschwitz was the German name for the Polish village of Oswiecim, which was razed to the ground to make way for the initial extension of the camp. Auschwitz II was nothing more than a death camp, built on the orders of SS-Reichsführer Heinrich Himmler, Hitler's deputy. Jews from all over Europe were brought here to be 'liquidated' and many of those not murdered in the gas chambers died of individual executions, obscene medical experiments, starvation, infectious diseases or exhaustion from forced labour. Above the gates of Auschwitz I and II was the infamous sign *Arbeit Macht Frei* ('Work makes [one] free').

The women's camp was part of Auschwitz II, separated from the men and the gas chambers by the overworked and overused railway line, which brought in many of the victims from all over Europe. The women had their own camp kommandants in Johanna Langefeld, Maria Mandel and Elisabeth Volkenrath, women who would not be outdone by their male counterparts in bloodthirstiness and devotion to the cause of humiliating and killing Jews.

A young widow, Langefeld had one daughter (though not by her husband) and seems to have lived off first her family and then her husband until his death in 1936, when she began her notorious career in incarceration and executions.

First, she worked for a 'Reformatory' that was in fact a concentration camp for women classified as 'anti-social' by the Nazis, ranging from the homeless and unmarried poor and unemployed to suspected and actual lesbians, leftists and sex workers. These women, considered so dangerous to the Third Reich, were amongst the earliest concentration camp inmates, and Langefeld, who had never held a job until her thirties, found she had a talent for terrorising prisoners.

This talent did not go unnoticed, and in 1938, she became a guard at Lichtenberg. Previously home to 2,000 male prisoners, Lichtenberg became the first formal concentration camp designated for female prisoners. Within a year, Langefeld had risen to the post of female superintendent of the camp, and remained until its relocation to Ravensbrück. In 1941, the Nazi High Vommand decreed that the camp must be 'cleansed' by the elimination of unproductive prisoners: the elderly, sick or those otherwise of little use as slave labourers. Langefeld personally selected prisoners for execution at Ravensbrück. By this time, she had been a Nazi Party member for some years, and must have learned all the intricacies of Nazi theory, including its enthusiasm for pseudo-scientific posturing in selecting candidates for liquidation as 'evolutionary dead ends' who would otherwise be a pointless drag on scarce resources.

Langefeld then did much the same at Auschwitz, having helped to first design and build the camp, which Himmler insisted include a segregated woman's zone, overseen by women. This contradicted Hitler's stated view that a woman's place was *Kinder, Küche, Kirche* – children, kitchen and church – and Langefeld fell foul, at last, of a bitter power struggle between factions of the SS.

Franz Kafka himself could not have created a more bizarre scenario. This woman, who had exercised a royal prerogative of ordering executions, was accused of 'excessive sympathy' towards Polish prisoners, and narrowly avoided prosecution on that charge. She resigned from the SS and moved to Munich, taking a job with BMW, until she was arrested for war crimes by the Americans in 1945. While awaiting trial in Poland, Langefeld, with the help of Polish inmates who had heard of her 'sympathy' for their countrymen at Auschwitz, escaped custody. She hid in a convent for over ten years, before secretly returning to Munich to live with her sister until her death in 1973.

Her colleague Maria Mandel was, like Hitler, an Austrian – sharing not just the Führer's nationality, but his commitment to the Final Solution. She was known as 'The Beast' for the abuse and killings of Jews under her command, including many children. She is said to have signed orders for half a million women and children to be gassed in Auschwitz.

Elisabeth Volkenrath took over in November 1944 as commandant of the women's camp and over-saw three hangings before she was arrested, just six months after her original appointment. She was tried, sentenced to death and hanged by the well-known British executioner Albert Pierrepoint at Hamelin Prison later that year.

Auschwitz III was a labour camp where the inmates were slaves to German industry, keeping the wheels spinning, manufacturing weapons, and manning other key industries essential to the war effort.

The main camps were around fifty kilometres from

Krakow with forty-five satellite camps, some as far away as 10 kilometres, with prisoner populations ranging from a few score up to many thousands. There were even women's sub-camps at places like Plawy, Zabrze, Budy, Rajsko, Gleiwitz and Lichtenwerden.

Those are the basic facts, but the full truth tells of many different horror stories such as the 'standing cells', basement rooms of no more than sixteen square feet where four or five prisoners would be forced to stand all night with no room to sit down or move about. During the day they were taken out and put to work with the rest of the prisoners until fatigue eventually overcame them, and they collapsed on the spot. Those who did not die from their exhaustion were summarily murdered.

There were also 'starvation cells' in the basement where inmates were given no water and no food until they passed away. These were used especially for those who tried to escape. Only 144 escape attempts out of more than 800 were successful and when prisoners gained their freedom, there was a huge price to pay. Their families would be rounded up, interred and put on show while ten prisoners would then be picked at random by the SS and starved to death as an example.

Then there were the 'dark cells' with no ventilation and no air where the prisoners eventually suffocated, often helped on their way by the SS who would light candles in the cell to hasten the dissipation of the remaining oxygen. Those candles were impossible to blow out, as the prisoners were hung by their wrists from the ceiling.

Auschwitz II was built at the demands of Heinrich Himmler himself as part of the Final Solution of the 'Jewish Question', the extermination of *all* Jews. It was here that two cottages were turned into gas chambers, called the Little Red House and the Little White House, the prototypes of other gas chambers required for the increasing numbers coming in from all over Europe, particularly Hungary in those latter months.

All the camps were run by members of the SS-Totenkopfverbände and the Waffen-SS with their chilling death's head collar patches, backed up by the Gestapo. The infamous Joseph Mengele, the 'Angel of Death', was based there and whispered stories of his experiments with children and dwarfs chilled the bones, while other doctors conducted experiments on the sterilisation of Jewish women and, even more horrifically, injecting women's uteruses in a bid to glue them shut! The women were also used for experiments with new drugs to discover any dangers or side effects, as the Allies had blocked German access to the opium supply routes, resulting in a chronic shortage of morphine, and Nazi scientists were given the task of devising synthetic alternatives.

Those of us fortunate enough to escape these additional horrors lived well-regimented days. Up for roll call at 4.30 a.m., half an hour for ablutions, and then we were organised into work details. We would be marched to our duties, wearing our striped clothes with no underwear, no socks and wooden shoes which were desperately uncomfortable as they rarely fitted.

We were not allowed to rest or eat while we were working and one of us would be designated to time the toilet breaks so that no one lingered too long! Incredibly, the Women's Orchestra of Auschwitz, a prisoners' band organised by Maria Mandel, would be made to play happy music as we were marched in and out of the camp gates at either end of the day.

Fortunately for all of us a further order from SS Command calling for the execution of all remaining prisoners was never carried out as the camps fell into chaos in the last days of the war. Many prisoners were marched away to other camps, many scattered and even some German soldiers shed their uniforms and fled to the countryside to hide as their world, and the Third Reich's bid for world domination, collapsed.

According to the history books those still in Auschwitz were liberated on 27 January 1945 which is now International Holocaust Commemoration Day. The liberators were the Russian army who fully expected to find more gas chambers after the discovery at Majdanek six months earlier, but they discovered only the ruins of four large gas chambers, as Himmler had ordered the crematorium to be destroyed just weeks before in a bid to hide the depth of the Third Reich's depravity from the advancing Russian and British troops.

But the murders were on too great a scale to conceal, and destroying the chambers accomplished nothing, as the retreating Germans left behind some 1,200 inmates at the main camp and 5,800 at Birkenau, including some 611 children. All could bear witness to the atrocities that they had seen. The last roll call the Germans conducted at all three camps on 17 January revealed that there were 67,012 prisoners remaining.

The difference is made up of the survivors who were taken on a Death March back into the old Third Reich, leaving behind the aged, the sick, the very young as well as a group of scientists and intellectuals. It is estimated that 15,000 died on these marches from Auschwitz in the middle of a cold winter.

Before they left, the Germans did their best to erase the evidence of their crimes, burning their carefully kept records, some of the barracks and part of the clothing warehouse. The latter was still aflame when the Russians arrived weeks later. They were stunned to find bodies stuffed in sheds, survivors who resembled skeletons and, of course, the remains of the warehouses that hadn't been burned. I read afterwards that there were 836,525 items of women's clothing; 348,820 items of men's clothing; 43,525 pairs of shoes, spectacles, toothbrushes; 460

artificial limbs and seven tons of human hair shaved from Jews about to be executed stockpiled in those warehouses. They had probably been intended for shipment back to Berlin. The hair, it seemed, was sent to a couple of German companies to be made into industrial felt or yarn to be spun into socks for U-boat crews and railway workers.

How many of our people died in Auschwitz? No one seems to know for certain. Rudolf Hess said at his trial that Eichmann had told him two and a half million Jews had been gassed at Auschwitz and another half million had died from other causes. He later retracted that statement and said that the numbers were impossible in the time allotted. The Russians maintained the figure was between 2.5 and 4 million but further investigations concluded that the real figure was somewhere over one million, including 960,000 Jewish deaths.

We had little food at Auschwitz and the future looked grim but then, suddenly, I was transferred to Bergen-Belsen, perhaps the most notorious of the German concentration camps, where 35,000 died of typhus, including Ann Frank and her sister Margot, as the war came to its conclusion. Another 100,000 died there, mostly by execution. It was reckoned that life expectancy at this horrific camp was a mere nine months and reducing all the while but, by the time the British liberated the camp on 15 April 1945, I was already on the move again.

The British were understandably horrified at what they found in Belsen with 60,000 prisoners, many of them desperately ill, and 13,000 unburied corpses. Before the month was out 9,000 more had died.

As one last desperate act the retreating Germans poisoned the water supply and thirteen days after liberation the Luftwaffe bombed one of the camp hospitals, killing patients and Red Cross workers. The conditions were so bad and disease so rife that the Allies burned the camp to the ground.

By then I had been taken to the Salzwedel camp in Saxony between Hamburg and Magdeburg. This was an ancient town, first documented as early as 1233, and, under normal circumstances, a beautiful place, but to us it was another prison. We were put to work in the ammunition factory, living in a sub-camp of Neuengamme concentration camp. It held around 1,000 women at first, but eventually there were three thousand, guarded by sixty SS men and women.

On 29 April 1945 the US army liberated both our camp and a nearby men's camp for non-Germans. It was too late for many, and the Americans discovered almost a hundred corpses of women who had died of malaria, typhus and dysentery. The US army turned over control of the city to the Russians and subsequently Salzwedel became part of the German Democratic Republic.

By then, I was away from the horrors and the grim

prospect of living under Russian rule, looking for my family. The Jewish Federation had provided me and two other girls with an apartment in Magdeburg. Then someone came to the camp where I was staying in Salzwedel to tell me they might have seen my sister Bluma, whom I had been searching for as well as my little brother Arie. I went straight to the camp he told me she was in, but there was no sign, and no one I spoke to had seen her.

The friend, who came to me in the first place, told me not to go back to my former camp because of the Russians, but to stay where I was and that a man called Nathan Shapov and others would look after me. He then introduced me to Nathan as a family friend. I was immediately impressed with his presence and strength and we became friends at once. That's all it was, we were just acquaintances and there was no hint of romance at that stage. When we moved out of the camp Nathan, who seemed to be very much in charge, made sure I had a room of my own in the Mayor's building and then told me he was putting together a group to go to Palestine.

He convinced me that it was not good for me to stay in Germany on my own, as there was nothing there for me but more pain and resentment. At the start of the war I had a brother and sister but I did not know where they were or even if they were still alive. I could find no news of them from anyone. So I agreed to go with this group of around a thousand people, following Nathan from Hillersleben to Antwerp in Belgium. We shared an apartment in Charleroi while arrangements for our passage to Palestine were set in motion. Nathan lived in one room with two men while I lived in another room with two girls. As it happened, he left for Palestine a year before me. He was sick at the time with a heavy cold and a high temperature, and I knew he had no legal papers for the trip.

A friend had come to tell me how sick Nathan was and asked me to take him a cup of tea with lemon. I took it over, knocked on his door but there was no answer. I was told he had been seen leaving early in the morning on his way to the dockyards. I had missed saying goodbye to the man who had cared for me and I was surprised at how upset I felt.

He left and I stayed in Charleroi. He was there for a year in Palestine before a Jewish organisation came to me and asked me if I was ready to go there. It was not legal, with the rigid British quotas on Jewish immigration, but I was young, I didn't care and I had no right or reason to stay in Belgium, where many people looked on us with some suspicion.

A group of us were taken to France where we boarded a beautiful passenger liner in Marseilles and I began to think how lucky I was. But once we were in the middle of the ocean we saw another ship approaching in the distance. It had come from Turkey, a coal ship and even from a distance we could see that it was very old and extremely dirty. Our ship stopped and the sailors took us down the ladders and put us into little boats before turning back and returning to Marseilles to pick up another group, leaving us to board and explore the rust bucket.

The ship was in such a state of disrepair that we were worried it would sink before we reached Palestine as it dipped lower and lower in the water. There were a thousand people aboard for ten days with no food and nothing to drink. We were so thirsty that some of us stupidly drank water from the ocean, making us very sick indeed from saline poisoning. The crew ignored us completely.

When we reached Haifa some jumped overboard and swam to safety, away from the British control points. The rest of us stayed on board and waited to see what would become of us. We were escorted off the boat and those of us with no family were taken to a military camp where we stayed in quarantine for one month. They were more afraid that we would bring diseases into the country than concerned for our good health.

While I was in the camp I discovered to my joy that my young brother Arie was still alive and in Israel. He had learned I was alive and he came looking for me. He brought a sack, pretending he was making a delivery to the camp and found me almost straightaway, to our mutual delight. He told me he was living in an orphanage and occasionally staying with a good man who was building a kibbutz.

Every Friday this kind man took some of the boys to his home. When my brother told him of my problems he immediately said he already had four children and I would become the fifth and he welcomed me into the family with open arms. I had lost all my possessions, but I had now found not only a brother but also a family. I caught a bus and was met by the man, his wife and my brother.

One day my brother told me the friends I had been with in Germany and Belgium were asking about me and wanted to see me in Tel Aviv. I caught the bus to the city with a girlfriend and my brother and as we were walking from the bus station I saw Nathan driving a truck. He spotted me walking with my brother and stopped to speak to me. I like to think he was looking out for me off the bus.

We chatted about what we had been doing since we last saw each other and he told me he was going out with a girl and thinking about marriage. I told him I would like to come to the wedding and gave him my address for him to send me an invitation. On that note I went back to Jerusalem thinking she would be a lucky woman to find such a strong and brave man. I had a boyfriend of my own, but Nathan had made quite an impression on me.

Sometime later, on a Friday afternoon, the dawning of Shabbat (the Sabbath) when one must respect the observances and restrictions of the orthodox, we were dressed up in nice clothes and sitting outside on the balcony waiting for the master of the house to come home from the synagogue. I saw a taxi stop and Nathan climbed out. I was surprised to say the least and even more so when he told me he had come to visit me.

There was no room for him to stay with us in our already crowded house and so he booked into a local hotel. I was very impressed that he would make such an effort on my behalf.

It was a short visit and the next day I went with a friend – the necessary chaperone – and Nathan for a walk before he went straight back to Tel Aviv. But he returned two weeks later, and then again and again, until his father told him he couldn't keep leaving his job to go to Jerusalem, and to be sensible and bring this girl to Tel Aviv!

NATHAN'S TALE

When I saw Hela again in Tel Aviv I knew straight-away I wanted to be with her for the rest of my life. At the time I was engaged to an Israeli girl whose family were comparatively rich, her father not only being a bus driver but owning half the bus himself – that may not sound like much, but these were times of widespread poverty.

After I saw Hela I started to have second thoughts, asking what sort of life I could expect with the Israeli girl. What if, in the middle of the night, I woke up screaming with the nightmares that haunted me?

It happened often enough. Would she understand? Would she be frightened? Was it fair on her?

I had a discussion with her, told her my problem and asked her what it would be like for her if I woke up sweating and yelling. She was honest and said she wouldn't like it and asked me why I would do such a thing. She didn't know. She didn't understand what many of us had been through, even though there were so many survivors around. I guess none of us were that keen on talking about our past and she had certainly never asked.

Her response was: 'We are getting married, so why are you asking me stupid things like this?' I told her this was not being stupid. This was my life. This was how I was. If she could not understand, I could accept that: she had never been in a concentration camp, and no words could convey what I had lived through.

I came to feel that I could only live with someone who had shared that experience, so that we would understand each other's nightmares. I knew then that it was Hela I wanted. I had glimpsed that understanding when I first saw her face.

I told my father of my decision. If I was to be a wealthy man, so be it; if my life would be impoverished, then such was fate. But I was sure of one thing: I was getting married to a girl I knew from Germany and not my Israeli fiancée. I explained how Hela and

I could relate to each other because we had been through similar ordeals.

My father supported me totally and told me to bring her to Tel Aviv to meet him. When they met he instantly blessed the marriage and we were soon husband and wife. Most marriages, they say, are made in heaven. I guess ours was nurtured in the hell of many concentration camps, and the mutual understanding of survivors.

CHAPTER FIFTEEN

BLOOD IN THE SAND

When I arrived in Palestine and joined the under-ground, my recruiters put me straight in the military. That's how the war that gave birth to the State of Israel was won: by people like me. People from all over the world who had suffered for no reason save for being Jewish, all of us determined to have a home of our own, however we achieved it. If I had to pick up a gun, throw a grenade, and kill those who stood in our way I was ready to do it. After everything that I had lived through, this was not about politics or ideology: it was a matter of survival. The Jews had been vulnerable for centuries because they had no State, no army and no means of resisting our oppres-sors: and now a third of the Jewish people had been murdered in the war. Creating a Jewish nation-state that could defend itself was the one way to protect those still alive.

Of all those who fought in the bloody wars between the Jews and the Arabs of Palestine, and the conflict with the British Authorities, the concentration camp survivors had more reason than most to fight for a home free from persecution. We were fearless. We felt that we had already been through the ultimate torment and nothing could be worse than the Holocaust we had survived. We were ruthless as a group, living by the Biblical edict of 'an eye for an eye'. The stories of my part in the War of Independence and Israel's early conflicts may disturb or even horrify a modern readership – after all, we hear daily of the plight of the Palestinian people – although, in fact, the word 'Palestinian' was not used in its modern sense until recent times and the creation of the Palestine Liberation Organisation by Yasser Arafat. Indeed, until the term was appropriated for exclusive use by the Arab 'Palestinians' as Arafat and subsequently the world media defined them, there were many Jews who referred to themselves as 'Palestinian Jews', whose families had lived there for generations, before the identity 'Israeli' was established.

In earlier times 'Palestinian' had been applied to any resident or native of Ottoman or Mandate Palestine, not on an ethnic or religious basis, and prior to the bitter struggle for Israel's independence, many Arab Palestinians called themselves 'the Arabs of Palestine', part of the larger Arab Nationalist cause, with particularly strong links to Jordan, who at that time governed the West Bank (they later renounced any territorial claim on the land, and explicitly declined to take it back from Israel). Whatever the terminology, the Arabs of Palestine did not want us there, and we had nowhere else to go.

But I came to Mandate Palestine as a survivor, determined that future generations of my people would never again be so vulnerable to the anti-Semites of Europe and beyond. It felt that in the battle for a state we could defend, any means necessary to reach our goal were justified. The concentration camps and Ghettos had not taught me to turn the other cheek – I had survived by fighting, and, when necessary, I had killed.

In the wars for Israel's creation and protection, I did things that may sound inhumane or worse. But now, more than forty years after the establishment of Israel, despite repeat invasions by hostile neighbours, constant terrorist attacks against Israeli civilians and international ambivalence towards the State over the years, there have been no more Ghettos, no more camps, in Europe or elsewhere.

In 1947, the UN had proposed a partition plan for Palestine, dividing the country into Jewish and Arab zones, with Jerusalem under United Nations administration. The Jewish side, led by David Ben-Gurion, accepted; the Arab side declined (which their current President, Mahmoud Abbas, has since admitted was a terrible mistake). War was then inevitable.

I was checked out very thoroughly before I was assigned to an Irgun Zevai Leumi (the National Military Organisation of the Land of Israel) unit, also known as the Etzel, the Hebrew acronym for the initials IZL, which even many Zionists described as a terrorist militia. They didn't like the way Irgun did business – but they did appreciate the results.

Initially allied to the left-leaning Haganah, the 'mainstream' Zionist resistance, dominated by the socialist followers of David Ben-Gurion, the Irgun had splintered off in the early 1930s, as the Haganah of the time insisted on a policy of *havlagah* or 'restraint', defending Jewish communities, but never going on the offensive to counter-attack with their elite combat division, the Palmach, founded in 1941. Many felt this was a self-defeating policy, that our only defence was a strong offence, and the Irgun split from the Haganah long before my arrival. Our creed was embodied in our symbol: a hand holding a rifle beneath the words 'Only thus'.

Our code was simple. Every Jew, we believed, had the right to enter Palestine, and regrettably, but inevitably, only an unyielding show of force would deter Arab resistance. Only armed Jewish forces could ensure the establishment of a Jewish State. We gave no quarter to those who opposed us.

If a Jewish boy or girl was killed we would find out who had committed the murder and kill them in turn. It was retribution. This was the dictat by which we lived. No terrorist was safe from us, no one could hide. We would go wherever we were needed to hunt down the culprits of atrocities against our fledgling nation's people. I have to admit those who called us right-wing terrorists were accurate enough with that description. We even fought the British, while the Haganah attempted to negotiate with them; in fact we would fight anyone who hurt one of ours or denied our right to a Jewish State.

The British hanged a couple of our unit as an example when they caught them. It didn't work; it simply made us even more determined, stirring bitter memories of hangings in the camps. Ben-Gurion's policy had been to fight the Nazis as if the British were not colonial overseers in Palestine: and to fight the British as though there were no war in Europe. But we took the fight to a new level of intensity. Everyone was afraid of us, even the British soldiers, with just cause.

Internal security was intense. There were small cells in each unit – mine consisted of a mere eleven men – and no one knew who else was involved. This secrecy ensured that if one of us was captured by Arabs or the British, even under torture he could reveal nothing about the broader Irgun.

We felt the British were more sympathetic towards the Arabs than they were towards the Jews, although that ebbed and flowed over the years. We attacked the oil refineries in Haifa. We bombed British offices in Jaffa. We did everything we possibly could to get the British out of Palestine. Our enemies complained they could not even go to the bathroom without a machine gun to protect themselves. They were right!

Whenever the British went into a kibbutz or a settlement and attacked or detained our people we would retaliate immediately, so they knew exactly what they were up against. We didn't debate the issue, we took action. The organisation was obliged to obtain weapons and spares for our outdated and damaged tanks and aeroplanes from places like Brazil and Argentina, all of which arrived in huge ships. The British seized the odd shipment, but the busy port was impossible to police thoroughly, and a steady flow of arms allowed us to keep fighting.

We always investigated who had put a bomb on a bus or attacked a car and then, when we were sure of our facts and had identified the guilty, we would go and take revenge. Our enemies came from those little towns to take our lives, so we went back to their little towns and took theirs. We were few in number but very effective and although we took casualties, the ratio of those killed was strongly in our favour.

Of course it was extremely dangerous and everything had to be done with great secrecy. But wasn't this how we had lived through the camps? We had become experts in the arts of stealth and secrecy, and had been in danger for so long it was difficult to imagine what safety might feel like. Oh yes, we knew about clandestine operations and mortal risk, we had graduated with honours in those subjects in our own university of Ghettos and camps.

When the Irgun planned an offensive a piece of paper would appear in my coat pocket, slipped in by a passing stranger. To the casual observer, it was nothing but a random string of numbers – orders were given in a code known only to insiders. Each message told us exactly where we had to go to pick up our weapons, where to meet up and, of course, our destination. We went on many, many raids against the Arab forces. They used to sneak in, kill someone and run away. We didn't do that. We would track them back to their base and then take them on, along with half a village if necessary.

We were the Warriors of the Freedom of Israel and I was fighting as a guerrilla until we formed a proper army when Menachem Begin, Jabotinsky's successor as our leader, and David Ben-Gurion made a pact and joined their two forces together under the pressure of the attacks on our citizens, when it became clear that the British would not leave without a fight. The new, unified Jewish resistance movement brought together the Haganah, under Ben-Gurion's leadership, and the two extremist groups, the Irgun and the Stern Gang.

Ben-Gurion wanted to control the fighting forces, but eventually the pact was broken and members of the two Jewish factions broke into open conflict once more. We were ordered to fight each other but I, like many others, refused, saying these were our brothers and we were not going to shoot at them. They were not the enemy. They were family. I was firmly involved with Menachem Begin's group, the Irgun, but being on the right did not mean I would take up arms against left-wing Jews.

Eventually, however, our fighting force transformed itself from a group of militias, often at odds with each other, into a legitimate army. Given our experience, many who had survived the camps were at the sharp end of the fighting. We knew what had to be done and we were prepared to do it.

The attacks on Jewish suburbs intensified and we fought back. There was a change in tactics after a group leading a section of the Palmach was ordered to storm buildings only to stop when the woman in command heard a baby crying. When questioned she repeated the orders given to her: 'Hit only gang leaders and agitators.' As the attacks on Jewish people and their homes continued, that order was, of necessity, rescinded.

When it became clear that the Arabs were set upon a full-scale war, the Haganah made urgent preparations, and in March 1948 called up all able-bodied men between the ages of seventeen and forty-five. However, within just a couple of weeks, Arab forces had seized most of Old Jerusalem, and laid siege to the New City where some 90,000 Jews lived. Small units of the Haganah and the Irgun held on stubbornly, but the Arabs clearly hoped to isolate and starve the Jewish occupants into submission by cutting the main highway to Tel Aviv. In a costly attempt to break through to Jerusalem, the Haganah sent armed convoys along the narrow, winding road, but they suffered extremely heavy casualties.

The road itself, now virtually cut off, was dominated by the Arab hill-top strongpoint on Mount Castel. It became a desperate military priority to overrun the Arab forces and gain access to the roads and our supply lines.

At around the same time, an army of irregular Iraqi and Syrian volunteers, under the command of the notorious Nazi-trained Fawzi el Kaukji, seized a number of Jewish settlements in Northern Galilee. Two Haganah battalions finally routed Kaukji's army, but not before he had spread terror all around, encouraging many Arabs to flee their homes.

One incident in 1948 made a huge impression on me. There was a small factory that manufactured cement blocks for buildings. One morning, a night shift of fourteen workers failed to come home. They were found on the factory floor, not just murdered but savagely cut to pieces by the Arabs who stacked these body pieces into one pile like some grotesque haystack. The Arabs were skilful with their knives and there were so many tiny pieces of body and bones that it was impossible to count the casualties, let alone identify them, and, of course, there was Jewish blood everywhere.

We knew the attack had come from Arab paramilitaries stationed in the nearby village of Deir Yassin. On 15 April 1948, we responded with a co-ordinated attack led by our commander in Jerusalem, Mordechai Raanan, and Yehoshua Zetler, the Stern Gang commander with forty of his men and around eighty Irgun personnel.

It was a brutal action that left many dead, and it convinced our enemies that we were serious, and willing to fight to the death. Many Arabs fled their villages for Jordan, Syria, Lebanon and Egypt, where their 'Arab brothers' were quick to gather them up in refugee camps. Deir Yassin was retaliation for four months of attacks, not just the slaughter of the innocents at the factory, as the Arab forces led by the influential Abdel Kader el-Husseini, who were fighting in the battle at Castel, had dug trenches and formed a local guard force with forty men on duty every night. It was hardly a simple village and the fighting was bitter.

From that day onwards the Arabs started calling us Devils, saying that true Jews would not do what we had done. Even the Jewish people were shocked by the ferocity of the attack and Ben-Gurion was openly critical. Many distanced themselves from us after our bloody assault: although, their official condemnation notwithstanding, the Haganah's Palmach strike force joined in the final hour of the attack, with an armoured vehicle and mortar.

Still, those of us allied to the Irgun and the Stern Gang were abused from every angle, described as barbaric and out of control. But nowhere did I read about those workers who were butchered, their body parts scattered and left in a pile, even today. I know it happened because I was there.

Our raid coincided with the fall of Castel, when the Haganah soldiers under the command of David Shaltiel at last won the long and bloody battle, thanks to a terminal mistake on behalf of the Arabs. Their commander, Abdel Kader el-Husseini, thinking the battle had been won, strolled up to a Haganah gun position which he mistakenly believed had been over-run and was promptly gunned down.

Shaltiel, on hearing of our proposed attack on Deir Yassin, had decided to co-ordinate his attack on Castel. It split the Arab forces and we were successful on both fronts. Within twenty-four hours the rudderless Arab army in the area began falling out amongst themselves over tactics and leadership. Finally, divided and outgunned, they decamped and set off to return to their own villages. When our troops prepared to launch a final attack they discovered that Castel was deserted.

But all this was forgotten in the aftermath of our attack on Deir Yassin, largely in response to an atrocity which has somehow been written out of history. What the critics had missed or failed to understand was that we came from concentration camps and had seen things they could barely imagine. Where were all these bleeding hearts when we were being gassed, shot and beaten to death? Our hearts were hardened by all that we had gone through. We didn't care. We felt we were obliged to pay back our attackers and we did so.

After that incident it seemed the entire country ran from us in fear. We were poison to left-wing Zionists and Arabs alike. This was the start of our success. Prior to our raid, the British had stood in our way with their partitions and laws but even they began to back off.

I have no regrets about what we did. All nations are built on blood: we distinguish between political and geographical maps of the world because the lines that scar the political maps, the borders, are not naturally occurring features like rivers or hills. They are carved out by human hands, and always, if one goes back far enough, it transpires that those hands bore weapons. For too long, Jews had been unable and even unwilling to fight for their survival: now, with so many killed, we were fighting for the future itself. Our means were vicious – as they had to be. American and British critics of our actions never understood a simple truth: Jews have long memories. The British had invented concentration camps in the Boer War and colonised half the planet, while America was founded on the near-annihilation of a native people. For the British or Americans to lecture Jews on the ethics of 'colonialism' and 'occupation' was so deeply hypocritical as to be almost amusing. Somehow, the rules were different, in their eyes, for us Jews.

I was lucky. I was never even wounded. Plenty of bullets came close but none hit me. This was what I had come to Palestine for. I came to find my father, yes, but my main aim was to help liberate Israel and establish our own country. It wasn't a one-sided war. The Arabs had some good fighters and the Jordanian army, in particular, were well-trained, well-equipped and well-commanded.

Latrun, overlooking the road to Jerusalem, was an important base for the British but when they withdrew, they gave it to the Arabs, and the Jordanians defended it for all they were worth. They knew the strategic value of the location and sent over their big guns to place on a high hill by the police station.

Our army mounted several raids on the stronghold, including two by my own unit, but they all failed. On the second occasion we drove in with our armoured cars and one of my friends, Gana Simantov, in the next car took a big hit from one of the shells and caught some shrapnel in his legs as we were forced to retreat. Simantov had been defending a group of wounded soldiers when he was hit. The shrapnel knocked him flat, and he lay dangling half in and half out of the armoured car. From a distance, he looked dead. He would have been, had the Jordanians suspected for a minute that he had survived but we knew he was clinging on to life, as he still had his radio switched on.

He was in a bad way. Everyone agreed we had to try and rescue him and the commander asked us who would be prepared to go in and pull him out. I had known Simantov for a long time and we often drank and played cards together. I went to the commander and told him I knew the man and wanted to go and get him out. He asked why a family man would want to do that. I answered it was one of the things we have to do – part of the Irgun creed, shared with the Haganah and later the Israeli army, was that no soldier, living or dead, should be left behind in enemy hands, as we have just seen with the long incarceration and eventual release of Gilad Shalit by Hamas – and that was why I was asking permission to do it. Permission was duly granted.

Dusk was approaching and offered me some cover as I crept in as close as I could and then dropped to my stomach and slithering forward like a snake, wriggling by hips and shoulders. Luck was with me, no one saw me as I crept up behind the crippled armoured car. It took me a long time to get there and by the time I was within reach the sun had almost gone down.

I called out softly: 'Simantov, Simantov, come on out.' No one answered. There were two back doors and two side doors. I went in through one of the rear doors and there he was lying in a pool of blood but still alive and with his gun, ready to fight until the end. I told him we would wait until it was completely dark and then I would try to get him back behind our lines.

Both of his legs were hanging on by pieces of skin. I found the field bandages in the wagon and somehow managed to wrap them around his legs as best as I could to literally hold him together. I took him under the arms and dragged him behind me as I propelled myself on my backside until I was far enough away from the Jordanians to pick him up in my arms and carry him back to our position. The medics were waiting for us and took him away to the next station for immediate surgery. He went on to receive Israel's highest military honour for being wounded so severely in battle, 'Hero of Israel'. Me? I heard nothing more about the incident. I did what I felt I had to do. Tragically, Simantov died twenty years on at the age of forty-two, blown up by an unexploded bomb in an abandoned army base in the Negev Desert where he was searching for metal for his scrapyard.

I slept for the rest of the night and then the next day we went in again and eventually we took the hill. Many people died in that campaign but we achieved our goal after five failures. The Egyptian General Sayid Tahar was given the opportunity of a safe and honourable retreat by Yigal Allon, leader of the elite Palmach militia. But after long discussions, Tahar chose to fight on and he was rewarded when his air force dropped supplies, including medicine and food. Tahar claimed later that his soldiers were more pleased with and lifted by the arrival of cigarettes than any other supplies!

With that success behind us the 82nd Brigade of the Israeli 8th Army were emboldened and we went on and surrounded Jerusalem – only to be surrounded ourselves. Once again a great many people lost their lives. I was lucky. For all the flying shells and bullets the only thing I caught was malaria!

For hundreds of years in Jerusalem they kept Syrian Brown bears and there was always water in troughs in and around the city for them to drink. We were hungry and thirsty and thought nothing of it as we drank the bears' water. That was apparently where I caught malaria. I was shivering and in a bad way and told the commander, who was canoodling with a woman, I needed medical attention and I told him if he didn't leave his girlfriend alone and help me I would drag him off her and force him to take me back to the base hospital at Tel HaShomer. He saw the look in my eyes, knew my reputation, and agreed. From there I was taken to Tel HaShomer and then onto Hadassah Hospital in Tel Aviv.

When I woke up the doctor asked me whether I was alive or dead – I looked so weak he could hardly tell. I passed out again and went into a coma. When I eventually opened my eyes the doctor was inches away from my face and he said: 'Mr Shapov – you just got your life back.'

Apparently this strain of Ethiopian malaria was extremely strong and often lethal. He added: 'Having survived this one you will now probably live to be a hundred. You are a very, very lucky man. Only once in a lifetime does anyone survive.'

Incredibly it has never returned and I am on my way to that special birthday. I walked out of there and told them I did not want an ambulance and would go home under my own steam because I didn't want my wife Hela to know how close I'd come to death, not from warfare but drinking with the bears. But I was desperately ill, in worse shape than I thought, as I staggered back towards my home, clutching onto walls to stop myself falling. It was too much and eventually I had to call a taxi to take me to my house. I fell through the front door and was in bed for four weeks, unable to walk or do much else.

What an irony it would have been if I had been killed by drinking infected water in Jerusalem after surviving all that had gone before. I let the army know when I was out of hospital and returned to the fighting when my strength had returned.

I was not worried for my life because I was not alone. There were thousands who felt the same way as me. We were nationalists and we were building, by force of arms and strategy, a nation-state. We had just come from a concentration camp. We all knew what that meant. We were the lucky ones, the survivors. There were many millions who had died in those same camps – was I going to sit on my hands and do nothing? Of course not! I was fighting for those who didn't make it as much as for those who did and I had perfect faith in the necessity of the struggle.

Hela didn't want me to return to the war but I felt I had to go and defend my wife and fellow Jews so that there would be no more concentration camps. Nobody made me go, but I could not leave the battle until we'd won some measure of security. Back then, I had been alone, with no responsibility to anyone but myself; now I was fighting not only for my country, but for the future of my wife Hela and our newborn baby son Mike, later to be followed by a daughter, Adina.

While I was off fighting on the front Hela was left to cope with Mike. Food was very poor, rationed and scarce. But this was something both Hela and I were used to, making our daily allowance go a long way. We were given a few grams of meat per person, so, while I was away Hela received my ration as well. We could buy potatoes and bread but there was hardly any other kind of food as the country was hit by famine.

I received very little from the government each month, certainly not enough to buy the milk and other essentials for my wife and baby boy. It was a hard life. I couldn't steal food any more because there was no one to steal from. We were a nation of paupers with little means, and, in any case, I did not believe in stealing from my own people.

By then we had a small apartment with one bedroom and in wintertime, when it rained, it would flood because we had no drains. We were fortunate that we were on the first floor since one night while I was away Hela heard a commotion and went downstairs to find the ground-floor flat completely under water.

Clearly they could not stay, so Hela dressed the baby, put on her rubber boots and went over to my father Mordechai's house where they were dry and clear of the floods. Someone let me know what had happened so I made arrangements to return home immediately. I would have needed a jet fighter to have reached home any quicker!

I took Hela and Mike away from our home and moved us to a deserted Arab village. The people who had lived there previously had run away and everything was empty and in a great state of disrepair from the fighting. I found a house with no windows or doors, but the roof was solid and would at least keep us dry. I told Hela to stay where she was and I went away in search of the wood and the bits and pieces from other wrecked houses to do some quick repairs and make the little house habitable.

This was the infamous village of Salameh, strategically built on a hill and a series of old-fashioned Arab-style house. Salameh was originally a stronghold for an army consisting of Arabs, British army deserters, former German prisoners of war who had volunteered to fight on the Arab side and a handful of Yugoslav and Polish soldiers stationed in Palestine.

These volunteers commandeered a postal services truck, filled it with explosives and drove it into the Jewish part of Haifa. Fifty Jews were injured. Two weeks later the British deserters stole a British armoured truck loaded it with explosives and drove into the offices of the *Palestine Post* newspaper in the centre of Jewish Jerusalem. The entire building was destroyed along with everyone in it. Salameh had eventually been taken by the Haganah.

It was not the ideal place to bring up a young boy but it was all we had and I, or Hela when I was absent, had to go downstairs with two buckets to collect water to drink, boiling it first, of course. Facilities were limited and there was certainly no corner supermarket. The newborn State looked as much like the modern, technologically advanced nation Israel has become as a horse and cart resembles a Ferrari.

Because the village was virtually empty it was unsettling for Hela on her own and she was very afraid at night thinking that Arab fighters would sneak in and kill both her and the baby, as had happened many times in those years of attack and counter-attack. I must admit that when I was there and heard the rattling windows I also thought it was the Arabs, so much so that I took out my loaded rifle and went off to discover it was nothing more than the wind and my imagination.

There was virtually no one else living there and between us we did not have the money to buy or rent anything in a more populated area. Eventually a neighbour, Malka, invited Hela to move in with her as she was also lonely and suffering from gruesome thoughts when she heard the wind shaking the derelict houses around her. This was a good plan as her husband was also in the army. So here were two families with no money between them because the army paid next to nothing. We were, it seemed, destined to go on fending for ourselves.

CHAPTER SIXTEEN

LEAVING THE FRONT

I had become weary of the fighting, the hatred, the death and the angst. It seemed to be endless. We had hoped, but didn't believe, it was all over when Prime Minister David Ben-Gurion, also the Minister of Defence in the newly created provisional government, signed Israel's Declaration of Independence in the afternoon of 14 May 1948 to the strains of our anthem, '*Hatikvah*'.

The British, tired of fighting a war on two fronts against Arab and Jewish Nationalists, had declared the ending of their Mandate over Palestine that same day. They left as quickly as they could, and now I am told that many young British people, often those most critical of Israel, know nothing of the Mandate, seeming to believe we Jews had come in and invaded a Palestinian State, not a British colony that had previously belonged to the Ottoman Empire.

The new country was to be called *The State of Israel*, chosen above other such names as Zion, Judaea, Ziona, Ivriya and Herzliya. The name was such a secret until the unveiling that the new postage stamps, printed prior to the declaration, were simply marked *Doar Ivri* (Hebrew Mail). Israel was the only name we could have chosen.

Amongst the signatories were future President Yitzhak Ben-Zvi and two future Prime Ministers, Moshe Sharett and Golda Meir.

It was an historic triumph but on the very day they gathered to sign the founding document, the Egyptians bombed Tel Aviv. There were no deaths but they damaged a number of our precious aircraft in the Tel Aviv airfield. On 15 May the British, apart from a small group left behind to supervise the evacuation, finally left the newborn state of Israel. But this did not bring peace – indeed, it marked the start of new hostilities with five independent Arab states lined up to attack our newly formed country.

The next day saw Lebanese troops coming in from the north; Iraqi, Syrian and Transjordanian troops from the east and Egyptians from the south, aided by a small group of Saudi Arabians. Israel, with extra troops recruited from the Cyprus POW camps emptied by the British but still heavily outnumbered, somehow held out until the first truce was signed on 11 June 1948, the night when one of our great military leaders was killed by friendly fire in Abu Ghosh.

He was David Daniel Marcus, an American soldier of distinction who became the Israeli army's (properly known as the Israel Defence Forces, or IDF) first General, known as Mickey Stone, to hide his real American identity from the British. They would not have been pleased to hear that an American ally was helping Israeli forces against them. His life story was later portrayed by Hollywood in the film *Cast a Giant Shadow* with Kirk Douglas starring as Marcus.

Marcus was a brilliant man who had served as an Assistant US Attorney in New York, prosecuting such Mafia gangsters as Lucky Luciano, and eventually served as Commissioner of the New York City Department of Correction and chief of the War Crimes Division.

It was Ben-Gurion himself who asked Marcus to find him an American military advisor to assist the newly formed Jewish army and when he was unable to find a suitable candidate he volunteered himself, with the backing of the US government, who gave him the one proviso of working under a different name. Mickey Stone was born, and soon became a legend as he pulled our newly organised military together into one coherent unit.

It was shortly before the ceasefire when Marcus returned to his headquarters in the abandoned Monastère Notre Dame de la Nouvelle Alliance in Abu Ghosh and in the early hours of the morning left a meeting of his officers to urinate outside, wrapping himself in a white sheet against the cold. The shadowy figure was challenged by an inexperienced young guard but Marcus knew little Hebrew and could not understand or respond, shouting back in English. When the guard fired his gun in the air as a warning, Marcus turned and fled back towards the Monastery. He was shot and killed by the youngster and other sentries who saw what looked like an Arab in white robes heading for their headquarters.

His body was flown back to the United States where he was buried at West Point Cemetery.

When the four weeks' truce came to an end, the war immediately resumed, until, on 18 November 1984, the government of Israel accepted an Armistice Resolution passed by the United Nations. But the Egyptian army continued its attacks, harassing the isolated Jewish settlements in the southern Negev Desert and bombing Tel Aviv. The Israeli army was forced to counter the Egyptian attacks and after ten days of fighting the Palmach, under Colonel Yitzhak Sadeh, captured the important town of Beersheba. On 7 January 1949, the Security Council of the United Nations issued a Cease Fire Order, and finally, on 22 February, Egypt and Israel agreed truce terms on the island of Rhodes. Treaties with the other Arab countries followed soon after.

Once hostilities were over, I gave up full-time service in the army and we started to look for a permanent home. Hela admitted to me it had been a really difficult time, as I had only been able to visit once or twice a month.

We lived in the near-deserted village for a year and a half before finding somewhere we could put down roots, somewhere in the suburbs where the growing Mike could play and grow up in as normal a life as possible. It was too dangerous to move into Tel Aviv, as attacks on buses and random civilians continued. We found a nice comfortable house where Mike could go to school and once we were settled Hela had another child, our daughter Adina.

I was very tired of giving everything I had, fighting in the army to defend Israel and rushing home every two or three weeks to see my family. It was then that I decided I wanted to leave the army. But it wasn't as simple as that – as an able-bodied man I was still on the reserve list, fighting when required and bringing up a family when I was away from the front.

Naturally I needed some form of income and with this in mind I rented a truck and saved up some money to try and buy my own truck. What else did I do? What I had done since I was thirteen, cutting meat for a local butcher. But I wasn't going to do this for the rest of my life – even though it gave us an extra meal or two we would not have had otherwise – so I took a loan and bought myself a truck.

Despite the peace agreements, sadly the fighting never really stopped and there were regular incidents to punctuate the so-called peace. Israeli civilians were often attacked by gunmen: as when a tourist bus, on its way back from the holiday resort of Eilat, was set upon and the driver, Ephraim Fistenberg and his wife, were amongst the ten dead left on the roads of Negev, surrounded in their bus by the souvenirs of their holiday.

Israel was finding it difficult to grow up and live in peace, and the blame always seemed to be heaped on our shoulders whenever we responded to Arab atrocities. Through the winter of 1954-55 there were a series of incidents when the Fedayeen, armed Palestinian rebels, crossed from the Gaza Strip and killed farmers in their fields and civilians walking in the road. Absolute innocents, but where was the condemnation of their murders?

In retaliation to the many attacks, our troops raided an air base, killing a number of Egyptians and two locals. The Egyptian response was immediate as they shelled Jewish settlements across the border. We hit back violently, killing thirty-five Arabs in a raid and losing eight of our own men. So it went on, tit for tat, with raid and reprisal following raid and reprisal, finally brought to a head for many of us when terrorists killed five Jewish schoolchildren and their teacher at Kfar Chabad, less than ten miles from Tel Aviv.

There was an added ingredient to the mix when, on 26 July 1956, Egypt's leader President Nasser nationalised the Suez Canal, much to the fury of Britain and

France, and banned Israeli ships from the Straits of Tiran. The Americans and British had tried to curry favour with Nasser's Egypt with financial assistance in building the Aswan Dam: but the Egyptians remained allies of the Soviets and recognised the Chinese communist regime, playing the superpowers off against each other. President Eisenhower hoped to test these alliances by withdrawing support for the dam, hoping it would strain Egypt's relations with the Soviets: instead, Nasser responded with the nationalisation.

The world watched, nervously, as matters escalated. Iraqi and Syrian troops moved into Jordan. Then, in October, Cairo announced a joint command for the forces of Egypt, Syria and Jordan. The Soviet Union's surrogates in Eastern Europe supplied the Egyptians with arms while France and even Britain, who had become our allies, joined our cause. Months of diplomacy had failed to break the impasse, and the allies, against Eisenhower's wishes, planned for military action – the British even drew up plans to invade Egypt and topple Nasser, but these were vetoed by their Army Chiefs of Staff.

The tinder was dry and just needed a match – provided by a Jordanian soldier at a border post outside Bethlehem when he opened fire on a party of Israeli archaeologists with a Bren gun, killing four. Four days later a Jordanian patrol crossed the border near Aminadav and fired at women picking olives.

One died and, later that day a farmer driving his tractor was shot in the Besian Valley.

War with the Egyptians in the Sinai Desert seemed inevitable and I, like all other reservists, found myself back in the thick of things once again. We were in a corner and, in many ways, the Sinai campaign came as a relief to most Israelis. On 29 October we threw down the gauntlet, surprising the Egyptians when almost 400 paratroopers led by Lieutenant-Colonel Raful Eitan dropped on the eastern entrance to the Mitla Pass. The Egyptians were stunned by the arrival of this fighting force, just 45 miles from the Suez Canal and 156 miles into the Sinai Desert.

The idea was to open a supply line between the Israel border and the Mitla Pass which was under the control of Egyptian forces. A group of paratroopers led by then-Colonel Ariel Sharon, who would later become Prime Minister, overcame three military positions between the border and the Pass.

Britain cleverly used the situation to demand that the Israelis and the Egyptians, who were in full occupation of the Suez Canal, should withdraw by at least ten miles from the Canal. As we were thirty miles away and the Egyptians were in total control of the Canal there was no doubting the true intentions of the British, as they desperately wanted the Canal opened up to their own and the world's shipping.

The Egyptians tried to retaliate by opening fire in the early hours of the morning two days later on

Haifa. Their destroyer, the *Ibrahim al-Awal*, fired over 200 shells into the city before being driven off by the French Destroyer *Crescent*. It went from bad to worse for the Egyptians as the Israeli war ships *Eilat* and *Jaffa* entered the battle, soon to be joined by a couple of Israeli fighters which fired rockets into the ship, forcing the captain to run up the white flag less than four hours after their opening assault.

The fighting raged on with the Syrians pledging their support to the Egyptians and we all waited to see who else would join in on the other side. Jordan was a particular concern and we were ready to counter-attack when a single shot was fired. But, within minutes, the Jordanian commander telephoned to apologise, saying it was a stray shot and not meant as an act of aggression.

The Egyptians were very strong militarily and President Nasser, a former soldier who had fought against us himself, came at us with tanks, aeroplanes and a large, well-equipped army. He was also over-all commander of the Syrian and Jordanian armies. My unit had only three or four tanks at the time, including an old British Cromwell without its big gun, which had probably been shot off. But we could manoeuvre the tank and shoot out of the turret with a machine gun.

Our tanks became bogged down in the sand when we headed for the Suez Canal via Sharm el-Sheikh and we had to pull them out with tractors 'borrowed' from locals. We were fortunate to suffer only minor casualties at Sharm el-Sheikh where 1,500 men were garrisoned.

In just six days we had fought our war and overran Sinai with a final dash of 155 miles along the shore of the Gulf of Aqaba while we came in via the Wadi Zaala where the sand took its toll on our vehicles. But we had stirred up a hornets' nest and the Russians told the Americans that if they didn't compel the Jews to withdraw from the desert and if the French and the British did not withdraw from Suez, they had 25,000 parachutists ready, willing and able to go in and kill us.

They never did like me, the Russians!

President Eisenhower, fearing the worst, gave direct orders to his British, French, and Israeli allies: 'Get those damned armies out of there otherwise there is going to be a war with Russia.' We were left with little option. David Ben-Gurion told us to withdraw to our base and destroy everything, leaving nothing behind.

We headed back but on the way the Egyptians surrounded us in an ambush that soon had us pinned down, with no escape route. It seemed inevitable that we would be overrun, until other units came to our aid and we managed to escape. But it was a hell of a struggle and when I returned to my home I confessed to my wife that I had almost died ... again!

There were just so many armies against us. We had fought, won our freedom and our country and now that was done I'd had enough and wanted to breathe some fresh air. I was not made of steel. I knew I might go into battle one time and not come back.

On 14 November, just a couple of weeks after starting our little war, the Knesset (Israel's parliament) agreed that we would withdraw from all of the land we had taken over in the Sinai campaign, under intense pressure from the United States. But the war had enhanced Israel's standing in the international community and the ability of our forces had surprised everyone. We had arrived.

But there was no such thing as retirement at the time and every month I was called up as a reservist, either to fight or to train. It was not only me but my trucks as well which were called to action. When that happened my business, naturally enough, went dead.

My son Mike, then a growing boy, remembers the 1956 Sinai campaign clearly with its regular blackouts, while I was permanently at the front and his mother scared to death. I used to come back from the fighting when I could and regularly brought the family food, meat, conserves, tins of sardines and fruit. No questions, please! 'Acquiring' food was clearly still a habit.

Whatever was happening in the war I always tried to put my family first and on one of my short breaks I dug out an air raid shelter in the backyard because I was afraid they would be bombed. I also fixed blackouts on the window. It was all very scary for Hela and the kids but I assured them they were only precautions and everything would be okay. I then went back to the front to carry on the struggle.

All this time the thought of taking my family to America was growing ever-more attractive. I knew that if we left I would have a chance to be a normal human being for the remaining years of my life. I had fought for long enough and it was time to go. If I stayed I would constantly have a machine gun at my side and hand grenades in the house. I no longer wanted my life to be like that. I didn't want a bullet in my back.

At some point the war had to end; the killing had to stop, if only for me. A real life was beckoning, a life without guns and constant death. I was getting older and I was a family man, with responsibility for my wife Hela and our two children. My whole adult life had always been in turmoil. I craved a taste of peace and, most of all, harmony. I wanted to enjoy my family without the constant fear of being attacked or called to arms.

I had spent fifteen years fighting the enemies of the state and then assisting in building Israel with my business and its contribution to the struggling young economy. In that time I had married, started a family and my life had changed. I had flirted with death too often. I felt I had made my contribution and pressed my luck as far as it would go. It was time to leave and, for the first time in my adult life, to live, without looking over my shoulder.

I had arrived in Palestine in 1945 and finally left for America in 1960. When we finally departed for a new life from the docks in Haifa, Mike was twelve and his sister Adina was ten. They deserved something better, I felt, than a lifetime of warfare and terrorism. I did not want them to face the dangers I had lived through.

Where else would I or could I go but America, where so many Jews had found sanctuary? There was certainly nothing for me in Latvia, no relatives, just a wealth of tarnished memories. I had no wish to go back to the land where I suffered under Russians, Germans and even my fellow Latvians. I will never go back.

While I was in Israel I received a letter from my surviving brother, Boris. He was back home in Riga and had been badly wounded, leaving him para-lysed and with only one arm. He didn't live for long afterwards, dying in a car accident, but death may have come as a relief because he was in constant pain and incapacitated. I heard from him just the one time. That was communism for you: no heart. He couldn't get in touch with me and I didn't know where to get in touch with him. Between them, the Russian and German dictatorships had decimated my family.

Although Hela urged me to retire from the fighting it took me a long time to persuade her to leave the country we had fought so hard to win. Our attach-ment to Israel was deep, and leaving our home was difficult for us all, but for me, life in Israel would always be overshadowed by the fighting and the wars I knew full well lay ahead, as the decades since have shown.

Hela had a sister, Bluma, in Atlanta, Georgia with a house and a business but even that was not enough collateral to satisfy the American immigration authorities. But fortunately she also had a cousin, Harry Litkie, in Chicago and he and his wife put up their house as collateral to guarantee we would be able to take care of ourselves. We were eventually informed that we would be able to make the life-changing move. At that time if you had a family member in the States it was much easier to get the papers signed. Immigration to the US is a lot more difficult these days.

Even then, with sponsors and collateral to guarantee our independence, it took all of four years to make the necessary arrangements and it was 1960 by the time we eventually packed our bags. It was the last of my many emigrations – and the only one I made both by choice and legally.

CHAPTER SEVENTEEN

THE NEW WORLD

With all our papers in order and Hela's family ready to welcome us we left Israel for America by boat, the *SS Atlantic*, sailing from Haifa. But nothing in our lives has ever been easy and as we were boarding the ship we were stopped to have our papers checked. Then came the bombshell: I was told we would have to leave Mike in Israel because he would eventually have to serve his time in the army. This was ridiculous, as Mike was only twelve years old at the time.

I argued that I had all the papers and documents, which had taken four years to acquire, but they were having none of it. We three could go but Mike would have to stay. It made no sense. Who would leave a twelve-year-old boy on his own, away from his family, waiting until he was old enough to go into battle? This wasn't what I had been fighting for.

No one on the docks would listen and I decided to take it to the very top and went straight to see Abba Hushi, the Mayor of Haifa, a man who had served the Knesset and his country well. He and his family had suffered many hardships and worked tirelessly to help establish Israel. Luckily, he knew my story and who I was.

He managed to pull some strings as the most influential man in the entire city and not only did he clear the way for our departure, he actually managed to make the boat wait for us until everything had been sorted out and came back with me to the docks to ensure that all was well. The *SS Atlantic* was supposed to depart at 2 p.m., but finally slipped its moorings four hours later with all of the Shapov family on board.

There were mixed emotions as we settled in for the journey. We all had our memories, private and shared, of the country we were leaving, particularly Mike, who felt sad about leaving behind a lot of friends and especially his football, a passion for which he showed real talent. I do believe I saw a tear or two on his face. We stood on the deck watching Haifa and the harbour lights getting smaller and dimmer, when, as though someone had flicked a switch, they suddenly disappeared altogether. It was an emotional moment for all four of us. But, as I told them, we could all look forward to a much safer life in a free country.

My father Mordechai, without knowing much Hebrew and without a lot of money had chosen to leave and go to a new country, Palestine. It was a brave thing to do then and now I was doing something similar, but could take my family with me, where he had been forced to leave alone. Hela and I were not the only survivors to marry someone who shared their history. It was a common and sensible practice, with husband and wife able to share the nightmares of the past and understand. It was a kinship, as strong a bond as blood itself, and something we held on to.

We arrived in America on 13 July at Ellis Island, New York, all of us impressed by the Statue of Liberty, but it was a grey day made even greyer by the tall brown brick buildings and towering skyscrapers. We changed our name! On arrival at the docks the customs officials advised us that it might make our stay easier if we changed Shapov to a more anglicised Shapow. If it helped us survive, why not? Many Jewish names have had adjustments like Goldberg to Gold.

We stayed overnight in a hotel in New York and caught the train to Atlanta the next morning, a modern high speed train with our own sleeping car. We arrived the next day to an emotional welcome from Hela's sister Bluma and her brother-in-law Zudek. They had not seen each other since being separated early on in the war.

The children went to bed, exhausted after the journey, but we adults stayed up long into the night, only half-believing this was real, that we were together again after years of separation and uncertainty as to who was still alive. We exchanged our bitter experiences, the different concentration camps we had been incarcerated in and the dreadful things we had all witnessed.

Next day Bluma took us on a tour of the city and we were shocked at what we saw, signs everywhere proclaiming 'Whites Only', on the buses, on the trains, in the swimming pools, everywhere you looked. Seeing these, I knew straightaway we would never make a real home in Atlanta because of the racism. The extent of it was terrible and it reminded me instantly of the persecution of the Jews, something I thought we had left behind.

There were even different water fountains for whites and blacks! It came as a shock to all of us; we were colour-blind as far as racism was concerned. In Israel we had many black students visit from Nigeria and Ghana on exchange programmes. Coming from Europe, I had not seen a black person until we were liberated by the Americans in Magdeburg. The Nazis seemed to hate blacks as much as Jews. In Israel, when I saw a black person I was always interested to stop and talk to them to discover their background.

Mike told me that he was eight years old when he first saw a black person. I told him I was considerably older when I first saw black American soldiers. The children were stunned by the depth of hatred between black and white. Mike went to a public pool and couldn't understand the policy of white children at the front of the bus and the blacks at the back – separated by a metal grill!

We arrived in Georgia when the Civil Rights protests were reaching their height. I learned that until the end of the Second World War the black Georgians were effectively denied the vote and were segregated in most areas of their daily lives.

While we were in Atlanta there were mass protests and a strong campaign organised by students Lonnie King and Herschelle Sullivan. But reform was a slow process, and there was violent opposition to the Civil Rights Movement. I was especially shocked by the Ku Klux Klan who reminded me of the Gestapo and the SS. The Ku Klux Klan were not just white supremacists but Neo-Nazis, viciously anti-Semitic and so far to the right that they made my old organisation in Israel look liberal! I had not expected such a group to be so influential in democratic America. It was not until after we had left, in 1965, that segregation and discrimination were banned.

Needless to say we didn't linger long in Atlanta, but money was tight, and I had to once more leave the family to find work and save enough to send for them to join me. Hela's cousin Harry Litkie found me a job for the Vienna Sausage Company in Chicago as a butcher and I worked hard cutting sides of beef all day. Before long, Hela and the children joined me in Chicago. I was glad not just of their company but Hela's nimble hands: work was so exhausting that when I returned home to our apartment in the evening my arms were so sore Hela had to massage some life back into them.

I didn't know a lot of English then, just a few words, but my good ear for foreign tongues stood me in good stead and I soon began to pick up the language, American style. We were starting from scratch once more with no furniture, nothing. Hela's cousin gave us beds and a table for the kitchen. That had to be enough to begin with, and we would buy the rest later when I had some capital. Times were still very tough financially, but, at last, we did not live in constant terror.

We had to clothe the kids to send them to school, especially Mike who needed to be smartly dressed as he went to the local high school. But they were fine and quickly made new friends, mainly amongst the other immigrants.

Chicago was a sobering experience because of the harsh winters and the fact that the American kids were standoffish with recent immigrants. Our children stuck with others from Europe, Israel and South America. The American kids seemed to think that the new arrivals were of a lower class. It helped in some ways because to get anywhere the immigrant kids had to be better than these 'native' Americans, (of course the descendants of immigrants themselves!), and smarter, and a lot of them excelled at school, with Mike doing particularly well in sport.

In the early 1960s, due to what was known as 'blockbusting', large numbers of white residents of Chicago, as in many American cities, left the city for the suburbs. Blockbusting was a canny exploitation of racial fears – real estate agents persuaded home owners to sell at low prices, sometimes even at a loss, because, on the winds of the Civil Rights Movement, 'they' were coming. 'They' could be us Jews, Latinos, blacks – it didn't matter. The population of whole neighbourhoods was completely transformed by race, while structural changes in industry caused heavy losses of jobs for lower skilled workers. Having lived in bomb-damaged houses in Israel and concentration camps in Latvia and Germany I wasn't complaining.

I finally decided I'd had enough of working for other people and although I was getting paid a fairly decent wage at last, I desperately wanted to be my own boss. One day after picking up my pay cheque I went back and told Hela I was going into business for myself. We had some savings and, with a little help, I was able to buy a small grocery store on 16th Street on the South Side of the city in a predominantly black and Latino neighbourhood. This was a much better state of affairs and even with my broken English I managed to get by. Of course, I had my own little butcher's counter at the back of my corner grocery store.

There was always the risk of being held up by the gun-crazy Americans and when a stick-up man tried his luck on me I felt so angry I chased him out of the door and took him out with a left hook. I held him down and shouted for my assistant to call the police. He was lucky I didn't give him a good beating, he certainly deserved it.

I would go into my little supermarket every day and it did well enough for me to sell it and move onto a bigger property in a Latino area. With a partner I bought a much bigger supermarket with a substantial butcher's section.

This was in a rough, tough area as well and I always made sure I had some sort of weapon under the counter ready for when the local gang members, drug addicts and bandits tried to help themselves to the takings, or steal cigarettes and alcohol. I faced up to them and pretty soon word got around not to mess with this particular shopkeeper. Business was good and we were so busy I even got Mike to come in at weekends to work the scales in the fruit and vegetable section, his first experience of real work.

But one day in 1966 there was an electrical short and my business was burned to the ground. Unfortunately one of the companies I was insured with went bankrupt, which meant that I received only half the money. We reached a decision not to rebuild as it would have left us so much out of pocket.

Mike was in his last year of high school and his sister Adina was in her second. It was Mike's dream to go to University and continue with his soccer career in College. He was offered a scholarship in Southern Illinois University but we wanted to check out California where we thought the conditions would suit us so much better.

We all agreed to move to Los Angeles in June of 1966. So we were on the road again, still with very little baggage, but there were a lot of people in the same position at that time. Moving State in America was much like emigrating within Europe, beginning a whole new life in a new country. We had to leave a lot behind because of the cost of moving it such a long distance. Everything was expensive, and often in Chicago we were very short of money.

I went West ahead of the family and rented an apartment. They followed on a couple of weeks later when the school year finished.

The move was everything we expected and we all loved Los Angeles with its sunny climate, clear blue skies and open spaces – a far cry from the Chicago winters, which were even colder than Latvia and bad for Hela, who had a heart problem.

Ironically, after what happened to my business in Chicago, I went to work for the Mike Green Fire Extinguisher Company servicing office and apartment buildings. Californian law dictated that the fire extinguishers had to be serviced once a year so they would be ready for use in case a fire broke out. It meant that there was always work and we quickly settled into our new environment with no noticeable racism and no violence to speak of. We lived in a very nice, roomy apartment and we quickly found friends who were also survivors, meeting them in the various Jewish social organisations.

Remarkably I also discovered relatives in LA, including Ronnie Felson, a female cousin from Latvia who was originally a Shapov from my father's side of the family who emigrated from Riga and changed their name in the States to 'Shapiro'. Ronnie's husband Walter was in the trucking business and he was reaching retirement age so he sold the business – 'Walter's Transfer' – to me. I was in the transport business once again.

It was an excellent move for me and we soon purchased our first home in the United States, later demolishing it to build a bigger, better building. That went well, too, and I soon found myself in the property business and enjoying my freedom like never before. We had a very active social life with our Holocaust survivor friends and we went on many cruises and trips, especially to Las Vegas on a specially chartered bus with around one hundred friends watching Israeli films on the way and singing Yiddish songs. Every holiday we would have gala events in different hotels from the Beverly Hilton to the Beverly Hills Hotel and we would donate ambulances to Israel, at least five to six annually at a cost of around $200,000 per ambulance.

This was like a dream after all those years of torment and tribulations. I kept wondering when it all would go wrong. It didn't, far from it, as Mike graduated from the University of Southern California in Physical Therapy, Rehabilitation and Sport Medicine after enjoying great success in football at the university and the Maccabees Athletic club.

Mike met and married Esther and has four kids, Roy, Dory, Ronit and Jonathan. Roy married Meredith; Jonathan married Ariella; Ronit married Paxon and we have four great-grandchildren, Maya, Adam, Ella, and baby Eitan, born in November 2011. It has been a remarkable journey and who would have thought we could possibly have had such a happy, fairy-tale ending.

AFTERWORD — THE SON'S TALE

Nathan Shapow, the man I proudly call my father, was brought up in the school of hard knocks. But though the title of this book – *The Boxer's Story* – describes him in a manner befitting a man who boxed and fought his way to survival, there is far more to Nathan Shapow than his strength in combat. He is a wonderful, loving father and grandfather (and now a great-grandfather), who for most of my life said nothing of the battles he fought and won, battles that made it possible for me to be here now. Dad never spoke of his killing the SS officer Hoffman in the Riga Ghetto till he had embarked upon this book, and tearfully revealed this dark moment from his past to co-author Bob Harris. Clearly the deaths of the two prisoners, hanged in retribution by the Nazis, have haunted him over the years.

My father has always been a modest and extremely humble man. Where others might have boasted, he kept his silence until now, though I know for a fact that he risked his life in Israel to save a General who went on to become a senior politician. When they met in later years, they would hug and kiss each other's cheeks. The General was showered with medals and honours, but Dad received nothing for saving his life. Yet never once did I hear him complain. To Nathan, he had volunteered to save a friend, and that was the end of the matter.

No family lives in perfect harmony, and there was, sadly but inevitably, some conflict between Nathan and his father Mordechai after the war. It's natural to assume that my father resented his own father's second marriage, and thought he should have made an effort to find my grandmother, left behind in Riga. How could he, or anyone, have felt differently? She died without her husband, the father of her children, by her side, while he lived in then-Palestine and built a new life. I suspect that there was lingering jealousy, too, brought on by Mordechai's warmth towards his second family. I always felt that the relationship between Nathan and his half-brother was lukewarm, and can't help but wonder if he thought his father favoured the new family over him and his lost brothers from Riga.

Still, as a kid, I visited my grandfather every weekend and Dad never tried to stop me or turn me against him. If there was resentment or jealousy on my father's part, he had far too much class to let it show. He loved Mordechai deeply, before and after his death, despite the fact that Dad inherited nothing, with everything going to his half-brother. He was quite a character, old Mordechai, and it saddens me that we lost touch when Mum and Dad brought us to the USA.

When we lived in Israel, after all his years of fighting in the War of Independence and Sinai, Dad worked hard every day but Saturday, when he would let my mother sleep late and serve us a rich breakfast of eggs and speck (smoked ham) with huge slices of Rye bread for breakfast. Of course, it wasn't kosher: Dad's love of speck went back to Riga, where bread with speck and vodka was a popular way to keep warm in winter. Though forever proudly Jewish, we weren't particularly religious. How could we be, after what my parents had suffered?

Dad was always caring and protective of the family. He didn't even let me have a bicycle when I was very young in case I had an accident, and I had to borrow a friend's bike when he was away. But he also taught me not to be afraid, and the bike-prohibition never stopped me riding – in fact, today, I cherish my collection of mountain bikes, a large BMW and a Harley-Davidson.

Always popular, Dad was a leader throughout his life, with many friends. In my childhood he'd often go to the beachfront of Tel Aviv with a truckload of neighbours. The name 'Nachke' was well known in Israel, and commanded respect for both his military career and his general reputation as a tough, assertive man who never suffered fools gladly. He loved the State of Israel that he helped to build, and often spoke of how he yearned for peace and an end to the ongoing conflict. In the end, I think he chose to leave for the sake of us, his family, not for himself. He figured out that once my sister and I reached the age of sixteen we would not have been permitted to leave Israel without completing military service: and he had done, frankly, enough fighting for one family.

My parents always shielded me and my sister from what they'd been through, so we would not be tortured by the horror stories. Many times, I couldn't help but listen, late at night, when I was supposed to be asleep, eavesdropping on their conversations in the way that children will – and I heard more than they wanted of the terrible years they'd managed to survive. At other times, I'd be awakened in the early hours of the morning by the sound of Mum or Dad crying out in their sleep. It tore me apart, as I knew that there was nothing I could do to rescue them from nightmares. I asked them many times about the war, and they would quietly change the subject or pretend they hadn't heard me. But sometimes, on Shabbat, the vodka would loosen their tongues amongst friends, and they would speak, with fellow survivors, of what they had lived through.

On another occasion, I heard my parents talking earnestly behind closed doors, when Dad had returned home with bright red scratch marks on his arms and face. We had no idea what had happened, and Dad brushed away the subject, but in the small hours of that morning, unable to sleep, I overheard my dad explain that he had stumbled across the man (the Yiddish word *Zhid* – 'lowlife' – leaps to mind) who'd swindled his family when they tried to escape Latvia for Palestine, stealing their life savings and passing them counterfeit tickets. I was scared, wondering what Dad had done to him, but later learned, to my great relief, that he had given the man a beating with his weapon of choice, his two fists.

Once a boxer, always a boxer. It was the vengeance he had yearned for, as that bastard's actions were the direct cause of Dad and the grandmother and uncles I never knew being trapped in Riga when the Nazis marched in. Sometimes, to this day, I wonder at it all – life can turn, as they say, on a dime, or a bad cheque. If Dad had made it out of Latvia before the war, he would never have faced the Ghetto or the camps: but then again, he would never have met Mum, and my sister, like myself, would never have been born. It was something of a miracle, in Mum and Dad's eyes, that they were able to have children, after years of near-starvation diets in the camps. When I came along, I'm told that there were great celebrations with all their friends and family. No wonder I was spoiled as a child.

You see? We Jews are not so easy to get rid of.

Dad went on to suffer several strokes, which stopped him driving, while Mum suffered the recurrence of rheumatic fever, contracted – and untreated – in Auschwitz. In her early fifties she underwent open heart surgery to repair the damaged Mitral Valve, an operation that had to be repeated ten years later.

Despite those of my bloodline lost in the war, we had a full extended family, for Shimon, the son of my late grandfather Mordechai and his second wife, married in 1957, and had two children with his wife Shoshanna. They in turn had two kids, Iris and Itzchak, who live, like us, in Los Angeles. Dad's younger half-brother and his wife died just two years ago, while my mum's younger brother Arie, also an Auschwitz survivor, found her in Israel with the assistance of the group *Hayas*. Arie had an unwelcome souvenir in the form of the number tattooed on his right arm as a camp inmate. That, at least, was something my parents were spared, a physical reminder of the psychological scars they bear.

Scars aside, my parents always loved life, and are never happier than when socialising with their many friends at weddings, parties and Bar Mitzvahs. I always loved to see them revelling in good food and vodka as they sang the Yiddish and Russian songs of their childhood. They passed on the Yiddish songs to me, and I in turn taught them to my children, so we could all sing them together, a beautiful experience.

But the most powerful songs I ever heard were those my mother would always be asked to sing solo at weddings in her haunting, melodic voice. It brings me great pride to be the son of such an artist!

My childhood in Israel was a wonderful introduction to this life. With such a strong and loving family, I felt confident and free. Football was my greatest passion, though my parents had other ideas of how I should spend my time, and sent me to study the piano with a Russian teacher who could be pretty harsh, rapping my knuckles when I missed a note. I played well enough to give some recitals and a few concerts at the age of ten, and my parents, at least, thought I was a child prodigy. But my love of football overcame my musical studies: my friends always felt sorry for me, stuck in the music room while they played football and head tennis in front of my teacher's window as I practised.

It wore me down, and eventually I started skipping lessons to join my friends, leaving my music notes at the side of the goalposts. This went on for a month before Dad went to pay my teacher, only to discover that she hadn't seen me and thought I'd given up with his approval. Dad was deeply disappointed, as he longed for me to be a success, and I was subjected to a long speech on how he and my mother had lost their youth to the Nazis, and never had the opportunities that I had thrown away. In later life, I made up for letting them down as a pianist, living out some of my father's own dreams as a footballer, and, having taken his advice to get all the education that I could, completing a PhD in Physical Rehabilitation, eventually opening up three clinics for injured athletes in Los Angeles.

My sister and I also took our parents' advice in personal matters, living life to the fullest with families of our own. Adina and her husband Mike have two children, Josh and Jessica, while I was lucky enough to meet my wife, Estee. We have four children, Dorron, Roy, Ronit and Jonathan.

While helping with the research for this book, I spoke extensively with two friends of my father's from the Riga Ghetto, Shulam Sorkin and Izzy Nussenbaum. Izzy is sadly no longer with us, but his book, *He's Not Coming Here Anymore*, has been of great help in completing this project. I met Izzy for the first time in 1968 while playing football for UCLA (I went on to play for the LA Maccabees in the Major League). I had only just joined the club, when, after a practice session, a fan who regularly watched us train, approached, welcomed me to the club and asked if I was related to Nachke Shapov. Surprised, I told him Nathan was my father.

Izzy almost collapsed on hearing the news that his old friend and mentor was alive and in LA. He burst into tears and told me that my dad had shared hard-won food with him when they were concentration camp inmates. When they finally met up after so many years, Dad and Izzy reminisced for days. Shulam remembers Dad's boxing days well, and regaled me with the story of his fight against the Latvian champion Herchke Zvi Koblantz, who Dad beat convincingly. In fact, it sounds like the match was a little one-sided. But, as ever, his fellow survivors remembered Dad not just for his strength and prowess in the ring, but his gentleness and generosity, sharing food he'd stolen at such risk to himself with other inmates.

They looked up to him in those dark days, and Dad always reassured them that in time they'd 'get the bastards' – as, of course, they did, when Dad toured Magdeburg with his American friends following the liberation, pointing out the most evil of their SS torturers, watching *them*, at last, overcome with fear, as the US army seized them and the tables were turned.

Of course, as the years go by, and my parents' friends pass away, they have come to feel a little isolated, attending far too many funerals as their circle diminishes. But they are proud that in spite of all the years of war and incarceration, they survived to have a family that is thriving, as I write, with children, grandchildren, and now even great-grandchildren.

Mum and Dad celebrated their 65th Anniversary on 6 November 2011 – along with Dad's 90th and Mum's 86th birthday. They have proved that despite being robbed of their youth and subjected to gruesome inhumanity they are strong, resilient people, who, when tested in the harshest ways, came through with flying colours. Their embrace of life and continuation of our bloodline is an inspiration that's defined my attitude to living.

It took many years for my parents to receive 'compensation' from the German government and as I wrote this chapter, my dad received yet another letter from the Germans, checking he was still alive. In this case, the reminders and bureaucracy required for the relatively paltry 'compensation' payments are not entirely unwelcome. Mum and Dad will take that money for as long as they live, and let no one say they don't deserve it: least of all in Nathan Shapow's hearing! He may be in his nineties, but I wouldn't want to be on the receiving end of that famous left hook.

Still, the 'reparations' payments are a constant reminder of the dreadful past. Let this book serve as the sworn testimony of we who cannot forget, that those who deny or belittle the Holocaust are nothing but fools, liars and, all too often, Neo-Nazis. As co-author Bob Harris wrote, this book may boggle the mind and imagination, its contents as incredible as the most outlandish fiction: but they are the truth, the products not of art, but cold, bloody realities that it is a sacred duty to remember. Never give up: and never forget.

L'Chaim! (To life!)
Mike Shapow